I will have Mind Healthy and in everything

Dealing With What Life Throws At You

*How life's trials can lead us
to a greater intimacy with Jesus*

Barney Coombs

that I achive

Sovereign World

Sovereign World Ltd
PO Box 777
Tonbridge
Kent TN11 9XT
England

ISBN 1 85240 397 7

Cover design by CCD, www.ccdgroup.co.uk
Typeset by CRB Associates, Reepham, Norfolk
Printed in the United States of America

Contents

Dedication

To the memory of Arthur Wallis, who I highly esteemed as a spiritual father and friend and whose preaching, writings and example have inspired, challenged and encouraged me in my walk with the Lord.

Acknowledgements

I always admire those people who are able to study or write whilst surrounded by people talking or music being played in the background; unfortunately I am not one of those people. All of my school reports included the comment by the teacher: "Barnabas would have done much better if only he had not been so easily distracted." In order to concentrate on writing this book I have needed absolute quietness, which means that on many occasions, whether in hotels, on planes or at home, Janette, my uncomplaining and understanding wife has protected me from all unnecessary distraction. Many times she has made herself scarce or, with tremendous self-restraint, has managed to resist the almost impossible temptation of talking to me whilst I have been working. She is a saint! She is also my sweetheart of forty-six years and my best friend.

I want to express my sincere gratitude to David and Rosemary Freeman for once again carrying out the editing of another of my manuscripts, and to Mary MacLean for her editing and helpful advice in the writing of the first two chapters. Also to Gina Charsley, my reliable and hard-working secretary, who helped with the editing and was responsible for the final manuscript being presented to the publishers.

I am particularly grateful to Stuart Bell for kindly finding the time to write the foreword for this book. Stuart is the apostolic team leader of *Ground Level* as well as the senior leader of New Life Christian Fellowship, Lincoln. I have a great respect for Stuart, both as a man and for the quality of his ministry and leadership.

Finally, I want to say how much I have appreciated all of you who have opened up your souls to me and shared your pain.

I have sought to handle your stories with care and sensitivity; if I have come over as lacking in understanding, please forgive me. I have frequently been deeply moved, even to the point of tears, as I have reflected on all that each one of you has endured. By opening up your heart to me, I have been better equipped to enter into the sorrows and sufferings of others and hopefully help them a little, as well as point them to Jesus.

Foreword

Barney Coombs is known by many as a caring "father figure" in the church today. I personally have benefited from his wise counsel and concern.

This book reveals something of Barney's big heart for people. Experiences and illustrations of full years take us beyond theory into the realities and struggles of life. This is not only a book that shares all the good and exciting things belonging to the Christian experience, but points us also to the obstacles, pressures, misunderstandings and failures with which we all have to deal. Obstacles are faced up to squarely, with no glossing over real-life situations. However, this book is not "problem-centered" but very much "Christ-centered". We are not just shown the obstacles that the circumstances of life present us, but are lovingly turned towards the answers which are found in Jesus Christ. With sensitivity we are encouraged toward a victorious Christian walk.

I especially found the chapter dealing with those who have been "scandalized" very helpful. I found myself substituting names and faces of people I know and love into the stories from Barney's experience, and in a number of situations, fresh light began to dawn. I also began to relive experiences from the past which have tended to make me defensive and became aware that insecurities still have a way of rearing their heads. It is always helpful to know that other believers have their share of pressures. What a relief to know that we are not unique in our struggles!

The "ten steps to freedom" offer a clear, uncompromising journey into a greater intimacy with Christ. Thankfully, whatever circumstances we have to overcome in life, we can be assured of overwhelming grace and forgiveness, from a heavenly Father who is more concerned about our success than we are.

Stuart Bell
New Life Christian Fellowship,
Lincoln, England

Preface

The last few years have proved to be the most rewarding years of ministry since I first became a pastor nearly forty years ago. The reason is that I have never prayed with so many hurting people and seen such positive results.

As I have listened to people's distressing stories, I have frequently found myself weeping with them in their wretchedness. For this reason I have had to carefully guard my own emotional tank. There is only so much that one can absorb emotionally of other people's heartaches.

The thing that has impacted me the most has been the discovery of so many people who have allowed themselves to be afflicted by life's circumstances. There are numerous people who have carried unhealed wounds for great lengths of time; individuals who have been bound up in self-made prisons, in some instances for as long as seventy years.

I have repeatedly asked myself, "Why is it taking so long for wounded soldiers to be healed?" "With all the Christian counseling about, what difference is it making?" "Where does the cross figure in these sad situations?" and "Why is it that some people know they need to extend forgiveness, but still refuse to do it?"

The following chapters are designed to address these questions. I have recalled many accounts of people whose experiences defy all reason; on a number of occasions I have even found myself weeping as I have typed the details into my computer for this book. Whilst the names and places have been changed, all the other facts are as accurate as my memory allows.

One thing has become quite clear to me over the past forty years of pastoring God's flock: growth into spiritual maturity rarely takes place through mountain top experiences; most growth is determined by how we respond to life's adverse circumstances. By and large it all boils down to a matter of making the right choices. Winston Churchill once said, "Great men are not born, circumstances make them." John Maxwell, in his excellent book *Developing The Leader Within You*, tells of a study of three hundred successful people such as Franklin D. Roosevelt, Helen Keller, Winston Churchill, Albert Schweitzer, Mahatma Ghandi and Albert Einstein. Of the three hundred, one quarter had handicaps, such as blindness, deafness, or crippled limbs. Three quarters had either been born in poverty, came from broken homes, or at least came from exceedingly tense or disturbed situations.

Maxwell went on to point out:

> "They turned their stumbling blocks into stepping stones. They realized they could not determine every circumstance in life, but they could determine their choice of attitude toward every circumstance."[1]

Paul Crouser tells in the internet magazine *U-TURN* of a man who turned an impossible physical handicap into a life of usefulness. He wrote:

> "Many years ago in my InterVarsity Christian Fellowship days, our particular group went regularly to entertain and minister to a ward of polio victims. In one of the beds of this ward was a middle-aged man who had no arms or legs and couldn't breathe for himself. Despite such horrendous disadvantages, he was cheerful and industrious, occupying a paying job for the local newspapers checking for and recording typographical and grammatical errors. With a small baton that he held between his teeth he was able to turn pages, reporting the errors verbally into a tape recorder activated by his chin. This man greatly enjoyed our conversation and participated as well as he could in the songs we sang. He was an Overcomer par excellence. Whenever the vagaries of life weigh me down, I remember him."[2]

[1] John C. Maxwell, *Developing the Leader Within You*, Thomas Nelson, 1998.
[2] Ref. www.u-turn.net

The challenges of life are constantly demanding us to make choices. If we make the right ones, fruitfulness and fulfillment will eventually come our way, but even if we failed to reap a reward in this life, we are guaranteed a rich one in the life to come. Paul, writing about his string of calamities to the Corinthians in the second epistle 4:17, said:

> *"For momentary, light affliction is producing for us an eternal weight of glory far beyond all comparison."*

However, if we make a carnal response, we inevitably walk into our own self-built prison and slowly waste away.

Unless we choose to break out from our self-induced confinement, we are consigned to the appalling misery of constantly viewing the whole of life through pessimistic, judgmental eyes. We end up consumed with its injustice, unfairness, unrighteousness and man's inhumanity to man.

The purpose of this book is fourfold: first, I hope to help those who have been wasting their life away in self-made prisons and who have become inordinately absorbed with their problems. By the use of Scripture and real life illustrations I want to help such people recognize the true state they are in. For, like the alcoholic, they will never find freedom until they first acknowledge they are trapped.

Second, I will endeavor to show that the only answer to all of life's problems is found in the Lord Jesus Christ. We need to fix our eyes on Jesus, the author and perfecter of our faith (Hebrews 12:2). Then we need to obey His commands. Jesus said,

> *"If you love me, you will obey what I command."*
> (John 14:15 NIV)

Psalm 19:7 tells us:

> *"The law of the LORD is perfect, restoring the soul."*

This needs to be coupled with fearing the Lord.

> *"Fear the LORD and turn away from evil.*
> *It will be healing to your body*
> *And refreshment to your bones."*   (Proverbs 3:7–8)

Third, I wish to demonstrate that most of the complications that arise following negative experiences occur because we make wrong choices. If it was a wrong choice that got us into the spider's web, then it will be a right choice that will get us out. For those who are in danger of getting trapped, it will be by making the right choice that we will avoid being ensnared.

Fourth, I desire to establish the fact that embracing the cross, sharing in Jesus' sufferings, experiencing endurance, denial, persecution, rejection, betrayal and even death are part of the believer's normal Christian life.

I pray that many of you who take the trouble to read the following chapters will discover in the person of Jesus and through His word, the glorious truths that, *"If therefore the Son shall make you free, you shall be free indeed"* (John 8:36 KJV), and, in the same chapter, verse 32: *"and you shall know the truth, and the truth shall make you free."*

Chapter 1

Failure, a Step to Success

"The best laid schemes o' mice an' men gang aft agley"
(Robert Burns)

Let us settle one issue before we go any further: failure is inevitable, no matter how careful we may be. We may adopt the best proven back-up systems money can buy; we may take diligent care in delegating responsibility to the most gifted, trusted person one could wish to find. But no matter how careful we may be, the fact is plans do go wrong. We can fast and pray until all we can see in the mirror is skin and bone, but it still will not guarantee the absence of failure.

The proper handling of failure is almost a prerequisite to becoming mature. To put it another way, failure is part of the maturing process. I read somewhere, "If the truth were known, most successes are built on a multitude of failures."

Many famous leaders who have since become legends did not start out successful. Take for, instance, the dubious history of Abraham Lincoln:

1831 – He failed in business
1832 – He was defeated for the legislature
1833 – Again he failed in business
1834 – He was elected to legislature
1835 – His sweetheart died
1836 – He suffered a nervous breakdown
1838 – He was defeated for speaker
1840 – He was defeated for elector
1843 – He was defeated for Congress
1846 – He was elected to Congress
1848 – He was defeated for Congress, for the second time

1855 – He was defeated for Senate
1856 – He was defeated for Vice-President
1858 – He was again defeated for Senate
1860 – He was elected President

Albert Einstein was so backward in learning to talk that his parents regarded him as abnormal and his school teachers referred to him as "a misfit". At school the other children went out of their way to avoid him and hardly anyone ever invited him to play with them. To make matters worse, he also failed his first college entrance exam.

Walt Disney experienced several financial failures before he succeeded with his famous animal cartoons.

Surely, someone like Winston Churchill must have been always a success? History will remember him as an outstanding man of uncommon valor, and a high achiever. So he was, but he was not a success at school. He talked with a stutter and a lisp and he did poorly in his school work. At the age of twelve he became a pupil of Harrow. He began as the lowest boy in the class and in that unhappy position he stayed. At the age of eighteen, Winston entered the Royal Military College at Sandhurst, but not before he had failed the entrance examination twice. In 1899 in the General Election, standing as the Conservative candidate for Oldham, he lost.

In 1911 Churchill was appointed the First Lord of the Admiralty. During the beginning of the First World War in 1915, as the First Lord, he urged an attack on the Dardanelles and the Gallipoli Peninsula, both controlled by Turkey. If successful, the attack would have opened a route to the Black Sea. This would have allowed aid to have been sent to Russia who was Britain's ally. The campaign turned out to be a total disaster and Churchill took the blame. He resigned from the Admiralty and regarded himself as a political failure. He told a close friend, "I am finished." In November 1915, he joined the British Army fighting in France. Such were the inhuman conditions in the water-logged trenches of France, that he became deeply depressed and came perilously close to throwing in the towel and deserting, for which the penalty was execution. He wrote a most pathetic letter to his beloved Clementine, complaining of his plight and how he was thinking of quitting. In her reply, she included the famous poem by Christina Rossetti:

"Does the road wind up the hill all the way?
Yes to the very end!
Will the day's journey take the whole long day?
From morn to night my friend."

Her letter was Winston's salvation. His spirits were revived and he went on to be promoted to the rank of lieutenant colonel and was given the command of a battalion of the 6th Royal Scots Fusiliers.

Over twenty years later, on the evening of Friday, May 10, 1940, King George VI sent for Winston Churchill and invited him to form a new government. Winston was later to record in his memoirs, "I felt as if I were walking with Destiny and that all my past life had been a preparation for this hour and for this trial."

Dame Agatha Christie wrote eighty-three books of detective and mystery fiction. So far, they have sold over five hundred million copies. She also wrote sixteen plays including *The Mousetrap*, which is the longest running play in the history of the theatre. Yet, when she wrote her first novel entitled *The Mysterious Affair at Styles*, which featured the famous detective Hercule Poirot, none of the main publishing houses were willing to publish it until finally, it reached the company, The Bodley Head, a little known publishing house owned by John Lane. The rest is history!

Playing it Safe Spells Mediocrity

One of my favorite Bible verses is Proverbs 14:4, *"Where no oxen are, the manger is clean."*

Those who achieve major success have usually made some outstanding *faux pas*. Take, for instance, one of my best friends, Bruce. Back in 1969 he was the church secretary at Basingstoke Baptist Church when I was its Pastor. One Sunday morning he climbed up the steps into the pulpit to give the notices. As he went to pass me, he bent over and whispered in my ear, "I'm going to launch out into the deep, brother. Are you with me?" Like a fool, I quickly responded, "Absolutely." Yet I didn't have the faintest idea what he was about to do.

Now, visiting us that morning for the first time was a young lady who was blind. Bruce completed the notices and, much to everyone's amazement, requested her to come and stand at the front and face the congregation. I could sense my hands and forehead beginning to feel clammy. I was grateful for the high curtain that stretched around the pulpit – it provided temporary refuge from the quizzical stares of the congregation. He then asked her to take her special dark glasses off. "As you can all see," he continued, "this young lady is blind. I believe God has shown me that we are to pray for her during our evening meeting. When we do, God will heal her." Bruce gave me a nervous smile and quickly returned to his seat. Suddenly this heavy ten-ton weight seemed to descend about my shoulders. As I stood up to announce the next hymn I couldn't help but notice the stunned looks on everyone's faces. I remember thinking to myself, "Coombsy, what have you let yourself in for?"

It was difficult to fully concentrate on my message that morning. All I could think about was, what are we going to do tonight?

Well, as I had suspected, the place was packed that evening. We did pray for her just as Bruce had promised, following which we tested to see if she could see anything, but it was a failure. Bruce was extremely disappointed as well as embarrassed and, if he had decided never again to pray for another living soul to be healed, it would have been perfectly understandable. But he refused to crawl into a hole. Since that evening I am personally aware of scores of people who have received miraculous healings and deliverances through Bruce's personal ministry.

The most striking example concerned Tom Oyuka, an out-standing Ugandan medical research scientist who was admitted to a London Hospital for open-heart surgery. Within two days of his operation the stitches burst. The surgeon who was caring for Tom finally told him there was nothing else he could do. News traveled back to Uganda where the state radio broadcast on their national news program that, in fact, Dr Tom Oyuka, the former head of Ugandan Cancer Research, had died following heart surgery in the UK. But they were premature.

On receiving this depressing prognosis from the surgeon, Tom sent word to Basingstoke Community Church, where he had close friends, requesting that the elders come and anoint him with oil and pray for his healing. Bruce and David Downer set out for the hospital immediately. All along the journey Bruce was asking the Lord for direction. The Lord began to impress on him that Tom's condition was a result of curses put on him back in Uganda. When Bruce and David arrived they quickly asked Tom if he was aware of any people back home who might have cursed him. His eyes lit up in recognition as it all came back to him. He was able to recount quite vividly three separate instances. Bruce and David reminded Tom of the words of Jesus: "Bless them that curse you." For the next five minutes Tom poured out blessing upon blessing towards these people. They then anointed him with oil and prayed the prayer of faith. Immediately God's power fell on him and he was instantly healed. Within a few days, he was so fit and strong he was jumping up and down in the sea at Bournemouth.

In the book *Rees Howells: Intercessor*[3] the story is told of how Mr Howells announced to everyone his conviction that God would heal a desperately sick woman who was suffering from consumption. The doctor had given up on her and she was expected to die. It all started with the woman informing her friends that the Great Physician had told her she was to be healed. She then shared this experience with Rees Howells and questioned him as to whether the Lord had revealed anything to him, but he replied that the Lord had not. In fact, up to this moment in time, he had not received any direction to pray for the sick. Four days later, as he waited before the Lord, he felt the Holy Spirit direct him to take up prayer for her by giving him Numbers 12:13: *"Heal her now, O God, I beseech thee"* (KJV), together with the verse from John 15:7, *"If you abide in me, and my words abide in you, ask whatever you wish, and it will be done for you."*

Mr Howells reported back to the lady that he had now received the Lord's promise of healing for her. Word spread like wildfire throughout the village and people's interest reached fever pitch as they anticipated this challenge of faith. Three months later she died. Some time later he wrote, "As far as the healing was concerned, I was to walk it as a failure and not make a word of defense. All the district knew I was praying for this woman's healing and now I had failed openly."

Undeterred, Rees Howells refused to give up and actually took part in the funeral. Hundreds of people gathered, chiefly because

[3] Norman Percy Grubb, *Rees Howells: Intercessor*, CLC, reissue edition 1997.

she had become the object of much interest due to the anticipated healing. The minister who officiated at the funeral did not
take too kindly to Rees Howells and used the occasion to attack
and undermine his ministry. He took as his reading Job 13:1–4,

> *"Behold, my eye has seen all this,*
> *My ear has heard and understood it.*
> *What you know I also know;*
> *I am not inferior to you.*
> *But I would speak to the Almighty,*
> *And I desire to argue with God.*
> *But you smear with lies."*

In the KJV verse 4 reads:

> *"But you are forgers of lies. You are all worthless physicians.*
> *O that you would altogether hold your peace."*

Clearly the clergyman endeavored to make him look an absolute
fool.

After he had concluded his part in the service, Rees Howells
then added a few words of his own. He reminded the people
of the great change that had taken place in this woman's life
since the Howells had come to the village. He pointed out how
she had triumphed over death, how she had seen the Lord come
to receive her, and how before she died she had said goodbye to
all those gathered around her bed. He went on to say: "Have you
ever heard of a person who is dying, shaking hands with everyone, as though she is going on a journey?" The people broke out
into singing. In fact, they became so joyful they began to wave
their handkerchiefs. Rees Howells said, "The sad grave was
turned to be the gate of heaven and from that funeral we had
the beginning of resurrection life in the mission. It was after
this that the Holy Ghost revealed why it had been necessary to
take this case – *'that no flesh should glory in his presence'*. It is death
first, then resurrection."

Even Jesus Knew Failure

When Jesus returned to His home town accompanied by His
disciples, He visited the synagogue and taught on the Sabbath.

They had seen Jesus grow up from childhood and His mother, brothers and sisters were still residing there. The Bible says that they took offence at Him and as a result He was unable to do any mighty work there except that He healed a few sick people.

In spite of raising Lazarus from the dead the Bible records, *"Yet they were not believing in him"* (John 12:37). Judas betrayed him; then when Jesus asked Peter, James and John to join him as he agonized in prayer, they couldn't even watch with him one hour, even though it was plainly visible that He was shedding as it were, great drops of blood. Later on that same night, Peter denied him three times and the rest all forsook him and fled.

Three years of unselfish, concentrated investment into twelve men by the world's greatest teacher would appear to the outsider to have ended in total failure in less than twelve hours. It doesn't sound like a very successful ministry, does it? At least, that's how the two disciples who were walking on the road to Emmaus viewed it. They were traveling the seven miles back from Jerusalem to their home village feeling discouraged and disillusioned. Three days previously, all their hopes and dreams had vanished in one awful hour. Their leader and hero had been publicly vilified and made an object of mockery and scorn. Finally, stripped naked and wearing a crown of thorns with the vile spittle of men running down his beard he was crucified between two criminals. There was no useful reason why they should wait around in Jerusalem, so with heavy hearts they made their way home. Then Jesus, disguised as a stranger came alongside and joined them on the rest of their journey. Immediately they began to talk with Him about all that had taken place in Jerusalem and how the chief priests and rulers had delivered Jesus up to be crucified. Their hopelessness and sense of failure was summed up with these words: *"But we had hoped that he was the one who was going to redeem Israel"* (Luke 24:21 NIV).

The Pain of Failure

I always feel sorry for pastors who are seeing their congregation depleted. It is bad enough if the loss is job-related and a move to another town is the only option. It is even worse if they are leaving because they are dissatisfied with the pastor's leadership, or they dislike his preaching; but when it is co-leaders who leave because they are disillusioned and have lost confidence, then it can be devastating.

I first met David two years after he had taken up the pastorate of a slum area city church. It wasn't long before he proceeded to pour out the story of how he had left his former pastorate. The lines on his face, the look of pain in his eyes and the tone of his voice left me in no doubt that he had gone through a harrowing experience. Clearly he was still bitter about the whole thing. The previous pastor of the former church was well-known for his gifted preaching, his caring heart and an unusual ability to get things done. It was a tough act to follow. People, without realizing the pain they were causing him, continually compared him with the former minister. Right from the start he never stood a chance. To make matters worse, the senior leadership of his denomination had failed to stand by him when he needed their support the most.

It struck me forcibly that here was a man who was not free to get on with his future, because he was still bound up by his past. What a tragic waste!

There are hundreds of "Davids" all over the world. I meet them at conferences or ministers' retreats. They cannot hold a conversation for five minutes before they are compelled to spell out the raw deal they were given. It's like an obsession. They usually give tacit assent to any counsel you may offer, but as they walk away you get the distinct impression that your words won't make an awful lot of difference.

In the case of one couple, they had been sent out to plant a new church in a small farming town of about 8,000 inhabitants. A group of about twenty-five people eagerly awaited their arrival but, from the very first Sunday, nothing went right. They began to make radical changes unilaterally, even on the first occasion the church gathered together. The older people just could not cope and were soon complaining about the husband's style of leadership. It wasn't long before the church disintegrated and closed down. After a while they returned to the home church that had sent them out, but they never recovered from the failure. Their disappointment and sense of shame eventually began to take a toll on their marriage until, sad to say, they ended up getting divorced.

Failure Is Not Easy to Face

One of the complicating factors in overcoming failure is the inbuilt defense mechanism of what psychologists term "denial". If we are suffering failure and won't admit that there is a problem, then there is nothing to solve. If people try to help us without being invited, we can become extremely angry and dismiss their kind intentions. I have tried to help husbands whose wives are about to leave them and who refuse to acknowledge that they have a problem in their marriage. Sometimes people won't face the fact that they are hopelessly in debt.

The most common cases I know have to do with health. Fred complained of severe stomach pains, together with obvious weight loss. Even though he was strongly urged to see a doctor, he insisted that nothing was really wrong. By the time he finally faced up to his predicament it was too late. He died shortly after his first doctor's appointment.

Then there is the problem of rationalization. This is where we can find an alternative explanation for everything that goes wrong and, because we can explain it, we reason that we are not part of the problem.

I suppose the most frequent line of defense used is that of blame-shifting. Eve blamed Satan; Adam blamed both God and his wife Eve. Later on in the Bible we read of King Saul who blamed the people for disobediently taking spoil from the Amalekites. We have all heard the account of a couple having an argument when, all of a sudden, the husband accidentally breaks something and then has the gall to say to his wife, "Now look what you made me do!"

Someone has given the definition of relief as, "when something goes wrong, you can find someone else to blame for it."

Recovery from Failure

First of all we need to resist the temptation to blame someone else. Whenever we do, it always results in some form of loss.

The respect, trust and loyalty that people give to us is too valuable to lose through us passing the buck due to cowardice. Once lost, these relational qualities are very difficult to recover. They are acquired over a considerable period of time and are seldom extended to us instantly.

The most important step we can take in order to overcome failure is to humble ourselves and take responsibility. The Bible promises us that if we acknowledge our wrong, we will receive compassion. Proverbs 28:13 (NIV) says,

> *"He who conceals his sins does not prosper,*
>   *but whoever confesses and renounces them finds mercy."*

Taking responsibility for our failures will stop our critics in their tracks. The Bible tells us to agree with our adversaries quickly lest they bind us up. At the same time it will also draw out support and respect from our friends.

Some people make a serious error by determining that they will never again place themselves in a position where they risk the possibility of suffering another disaster. People who make this mistake cannot help but develop a hard heart towards God. The fact is, they are no longer open to hear His voice unreservedly. The parable of the talents is a clear revelation of what God thinks about those who fail to take risks. The one who buried his talent to protect it, ended up having it taken away and found himself in agony in outer darkness.

Three more things before we move on to the next hurdle. Firstly, we can never afford the luxury of self-pity. We need to treat it like the plague. If we don't, it can have a most destructive effect on our lives. Self-pity feeds our insecurity and sense of fairness. When this happens we are only a short step away from being scandalized, which is a subject I will address in a further chapter.

Secondly, never give up hope! Even if it seems you fail at just about everything you attempt to do, you could yet leave your mark on history. Take for instance the case of the Rev. Paul Kingdon. It is recorded in his obituary that he was well known in Oxford during the 1930s where he just missed a double first in Greats. He went on to take the Diploma in Theology with distinction after which he studied at Tubingen, where he was introduced to the liberal theologians of the time.

Unfortunately he never fulfilled his early promise. Although a Fellow of Exeter College, Oxford, from 1933 to 1945 he had no vocation as a teacher. *The Daily Telegraph* records:

> "He was relentless in the pursuit of arcane detail and lectured in terms so obscure that few of his students could

understand him. Sadly he fared little better as a parish priest. He had a remarkable capacity for creating misunderstanding and often left a trail of havoc behind him."

In 1951 he returned to teaching, at King Alfred's College, Winchester. Once again he was a failure and left in 1956. From Winchester he became Vicar of Chewton Mendip and lectured at Wells Theological College. *The Daily Telegraph* records:

> "He was quite unfitted for both these posts, the second of which only lasted a fortnight."

However, in 1958 Kingdon completed his history of the Church in Germany as well as editing and translating two extracts from Kittel's monumental *Theological Word Book of the New Testament.* They were models of scholarship and lucidity. This theological work of Kittel is probably the foremost textbook of New Testament words in our English-speaking theological seminaries. So in spite of all his earlier failures, Paul Kingdon ended his ministry by making a major contribution in the training and equipping of thousands of theological students all over the English-speaking world.

Thirdly, determine to be convinced that through all the failures of the past, you have been acquiring invaluable wisdom. Those failures can be stepping stones to success. Remember the words of Winston Churchill: "All my past life had been a preparation for this hour and for this trial."

Don't waste your sorrows, they cost too much. If you put them to proper use, they will prove to be priceless. I heard a story recently about Tom Watson Senior, the founder of IBM. He had called one of his executives in to see him. The executive had made some decisions that had resulted in a $20 million loss. On entering the office, the executive said, "So I guess you're going to fire me," to which the IBM founder replied, "Fire you!? I have just invested $20 million in you!"

We cannot end this chapter without the encouragement of Hebrews 10:35,

> "... *do not throw away your confidence, which has a great reward."*

Or as Winston Churchill once said, "Never, never, never give in."

Chapter 2

Trust Betrayed

The word "betrayed" carries such an emotive connotation. The moment you hear the word spoken, the name Judas immediately springs to mind.

On numerous occasions during the course of my life, I have heard the phrase, "I felt betrayed." In every one of these situations I can remember, there had existed a close, trusting relationship. The psalmist expresses it this way:

> "If an enemy were insulting me,
>   I could endure it;
> if a foe were raising himself against me,
>   I could hide from him.
> But it is you, a man like myself,
>   my companion, my close friend,
> with whom I once enjoyed sweet fellowship
>   as we walked with the throng at the house of God."
>
> (Psalm 55:12–14 NIV)

Betrayal of Trust

I don't think I have ever met anyone who at some time or another in their life has not felt that their trust had been betrayed. I know this is true for me. The first time it happened in my experience was in my late teens. I was a police cadet at the time and used to travel most weekends to a small town in the south of England where there was a lively church that attracted quite a large crowd of young people. In this church was a young, attractive married woman who was absolutely on fire in her love for Jesus. Dorothy (not her real name) was radiantly happy in her faith. She loved to pray and read her Bible; she was totally unashamed of Jesus; she would share her faith with others at every opportunity. In 1955 she organized coach trips to the Billy Graham crusade at Harringay Arena in North London. As far as I was concerned, she was the perfect model of what a Christian ought to be. I used to take other police cadets with me on these weekends just to meet her and to hear her testimony. As a result several of them made a commitment to Christ; one of whom was best man at my wedding.

One day the church youth group went on a ten-mile ramble into the countryside. After about five miles, the line of ramblers had begun to stretch out over a considerable distance with me leading the way. Immediately behind me came Dorothy and a young man who had recently become a Christian. I was beginning to get somewhat concerned with the level of familiarity that seemed to be developing between them and then it happened: I turned round to say something and there they were – there was no mistaking it – they were kissing each other on the lips! It can't be true, I thought. She wouldn't do this! But she was! Dorothy, my perfect model of a Christian, was betraying my trust. I was shattered. That night, my pillow was wet with tears. Seventeen-year-olds usually feel things very deeply and I was no exception. It took me months to recover. In the end I found relief with the thought that the only person I could guarantee would never let me down was the Lord Jesus.

Brian (not his real name), a close friend of mine and a senior church leader in the UK, became a Christian in his mid-teens and joined a Pentecostal church. The pastor soon recognized the hand of God on the life of this recent convert and took him under his wing. Within a year he was beginning to prepare his young charge for leadership. A strong bond of trust and admiration developed in Brian's heart towards his pastor. After a while, rumors began to circulate amongst the congregation that the pastor was having an affair with one of the ladies in the church. Eventually Brian picked up on the stories. His staunch loyalty and fierce anger immediately flared up in defense of his beloved hero. How dare anybody make such false accusations against the Lord's anointed? Sadly, the accounts were accurate. Eventually the pastor publicly confessed his sin to the congregation and acknowledged his betrayal of their trust. Brian was devastated. To this day the scars of that betrayal can still be found in my friend.

The Betrayal of Confidentiality

Then there is the betrayal of confidentiality. Failure to keep confidentiality has got to be one of the seven deadly sins of a pastor.

Bernard responded to the minister's Sunday morning message on holiness with genuine repentance and sorrow. He immediately asked for an appointment with the pastor where he related how he had broken his marriage vows a number of times by visits to a brothel. There was no doubting the man's sincerity. He confessed his sin to his wife and was graciously forgiven. A few years passed and the pastor moved on to another church. One day Bernard and his wife asked one of the elders for some counseling. All was not well in their relationship and wisely, they sought some help. During the first counseling session, the elder raised the question of how much Bernard's sin of adultery might be contributing to their present difficulties. Bernard could not believe his ears. "How did you get to know about my adultery?" he angrily enquired. "That confession was made in strictest confidence. Now I suppose everyone in the whole church has heard about it?" No explanation was acceptable to Bernard. He felt betrayed. Within a few months he left and joined another church.

The Judas Betrayal

It may sound strange, but some people seem to draw a certain degree of comfort from knowing that Jesus had a Judas. This type of betrayal is probably the most difficult to handle. This is because it involves one of your subordinates taking advantage of their personal knowledge of you, gained through their intimate relationship with you. It is not without significance that Judas betrayed Jesus with a kiss.

Of course there were no weak areas in the character of Jesus for Judas to exploit, but he did know where Jesus would be on the night of His arrest and for thirty pieces of silver was willing to take the Roman soldiers to the garden and point out to them which one was Jesus. I suppose we could define the Judas betrayal as: exploiting a position of trust to one's own advantage, knowing it will result in pain and damage to the one who was kind enough to provide a place for you in their team.

The story of Absalom is a classic example of betrayal. He took advantage of his privileged position as the king's son by offering his father's subjects a better deal and giving them the idea that they would receive better government and care if he was in charge. Like the proverbial cuckoo, King David found himself ousted from his own nest. I have met dozens of pastors who have suffered a similar fate. In some cases their assistant pastors have courted the affection and hearts of the church members and gradually turned the congregation against their leader. Perhaps a group of people have been gathering covertly and then without warning have broken off and started a new congregation. A well-known church leader and author once related to me how he had accompanied one of his deacons hundreds of miles to another city where this man was to sit an oral examination of his university thesis. The following Sunday the deacon was not in the service and nor were another thirty other members. He later discovered that they had all left the church to plant a new one. During the entire time they spent together in the car not one hint had been given that this man was going to take thirty people and start a new church. In fact, these people had been meeting secretly for months without the pastor's knowledge. Does that sound familiar? The pastor was not only deeply hurt, he felt betrayed.

I often feel sympathy for ministers whose churches are governed democratically. They are so vulnerable to betrayal by their deacons. One minister I knew turned up to chair the quarterly church business meeting and found that the "order of business" sheet prepared by the church secretary included the words "deacon's recommendation". He had not the slightest idea what this meant. Eventually he announced, "And now we come to the deacon's recommendation". Two of his deacons proposed and seconded that an extraordinary church meeting be called to discuss the motion that "this church no longer has confidence in the leadership of its pastor". He returned to his home that night a broken and demoralized man. He never recovered from the humiliation.

Judas or Peter?

The Bible describes the sin of Judas as betrayal and the sin of Peter as denial, and there is a difference. Judas, out of a desire for monetary gain was actively engaged in a plot that would result in Jesus being executed. He meant to harm Jesus, whereas Peter had no desire to cause Jesus any trouble. On the contrary, he wanted to fight the Roman soldiers and, in a rush of blood to the head, grabbed a sword and cut off the ear of the high priest's servant. In the end however, he ran out of courage, so in order to save his own life he denied that he knew his Lord.

Several times in the course of my ministry I have been on the receiving end of Judas-type betrayal. There have been people who have deliberately tried to destroy my reputation by spreading lies and half-truths or just dropping subtle innuendoes. I hope the following lessons I learned during these times may be of help.

Firstly, never defend yourself, especially from the pulpit. Self-vindication is the devil's delight. Once he can draw you into this futile exercise he won't stop. He loves to create problems that draw a defensive response in order to drain our emotional tank. This is one of the ways he seeks to wear out the saints of God. When Jesus was attacked, His reaction was to become lamb-like. This lines up with the prophetic scripture recorded in Isaiah 53:7:

> *"He was oppressed and He was afflicted,*
> *Yet He did not open His mouth;*
> *Like a lamb that is led to the slaughter,*
> *And like a sheep that is silent before its shearers,*
> *So He did not open His mouth."*

Then again in 1 Peter 2:23:

> *"and while being reviled, He did not revile in return; while suffering, He uttered no threats, but kept entrusting Himself to Him who judges righteously."*

If we are ministers and we use our sermons to strike back at the assailants in our congregation, we risk the distinct possibility of losing the respect and even the trust of our most loyal supporters. Whenever we minister out of reaction we can almost guarantee our motives are to glorify ourselves, rather than to glorify God.

Always forgive and bless; to do so then opens the way for the Lord to save us. If we try to save ourselves we end up losing, but if we cast ourselves upon the Lord and trust in His protection, then we are acting in humility and He has promised to give grace to the humble. We will take a much closer look at this in chapters 7, 8 and 9 when we handle the matter of being scandalized. One final word: when we fail to forgive and bless those who curse us and mistreat us, then we are deliberately disobeying the command of Jesus.

Chapter 3

The Wounds of a Friend

"Little people criticize, big people appreciate."
(Smith Wigglesworth)

There are two types of criticism: that which is constructive and that which is destructive. If we are to be truly honest no one enjoys either one. I have yet to meet anyone, who on receiving some negative words, immediately turns round and says, "That's the most wonderful thing that has ever been said to me in my whole life."

First of all, let's take a look at the sort of criticism that comes from people who love us and who only desire the best for us: the Scriptures honor this type of "quality" criticism in one of the great proverbs collected by Solomon,

"Faithful are the wounds of a friend." (Proverbs 27:6)

When I was a pastor at Basingstoke back in the late sixties, I remember one of the deacons coming to me and sharing how concerned he had become with my preaching. He said, "Over the last few weeks there has been nothing in it; you're not your usual self." It was like an arrow straight into my heart. I knew it was true. I sat silent for a while and then suddenly dissolved into floods of tears.

He was quite unaware of all the stress I had been struggling with during those weeks. Bit by bit, I managed to unburden my soul. It was such a relief. At last I was able to tell someone all that had been going on inside of me. He listened with genuine compassion. Finally, he came over to my chair and knelt beside me. Putting his arm around my shoulder, he began to pray and as he prayed he started to cry. I don't recall what he prayed. All I remember was feeling the love of my heavenly Father encompassing me. If anyone had entered the room at that moment they would have seen a strange sight: two grown up men with their arms around each other, weeping. For me, it still remains one of my most precious memories.

The next day, together with our two sons, Stephen and Mark, I traveled by car up to Scotland. After a while, I began to think about what had happened the previous evening. Again I was moved to tears as I considered what a blessed man I was to have friends who loved me enough to tell me the truth – friends who were also willing to take the risk of not only having their concerns rejected, but worse still, the possibility of our friendship being destroyed as well.

I have the unfortunate habit of "hmm...ing" and "ahh... ing" when feeling insecure. This affliction particularly attacks me when I am in the presence of famous people. One such occasion was the visit of the celebrated pioneer missionary W.F.P. Burton to our home. I always felt unusually nervous around the great man. We had just finished our evening meal when Mr Burton began to repeat rather emphatically, "Ah, ah, ah, ah, ah." Finally I interrupted him and asked, "Is anything wrong, brother Burton?" He responded, "Yes, you man, you!" Nervously I enquired, "Could you explain? I'm sorry I don't understand." "Well, you keep saying 'ah, ah, ah . . .', spit it out man, spit it out!"

As the years have gone by I have increasingly felt honored that one so godly and sought after would care to take the time to come and preach to our little Baptist congregation, but more importantly, that he took a personal interest in my pastoral leadership of God's people. I still cherish the benefit of the counsel I received. It came from a large reservoir of distilled wisdom, accumulated over many years in the ministry. I'm so glad I had enough common sense at the time to realize that this was God's precious gift to me and that I'd better quickly learn to receive with joy the occasional, good, old-fashioned, forthright admonition Uncle Willie handed out.

Correction Is Not Rejection

Before we continue much further we need to establish one important fact and it's this: because someone *corrects* us, it does not mean they *reject* us – even when they may be expressing their concern with a certain amount of emotion.

Criticism does not always come in measured tones accompanied by warm friendly smiles. Sometimes, we may have been guilty of making a serious error that has caused a great amount of grief. In such a circumstance, it would be totally unreasonable to expect a soft, gentle rebuke. It would have neither integrity nor reality.

I remember on one occasion sitting in an elders' meeting and informing them of an important decision I had made without consulting them. The atmosphere suddenly took a decided turn for the worse. I can still picture the face of one of the elders as his emotional engine gathered steam. It didn't take long before he let me know in no uncertain terms what he thought about my decision. He was angry, there was no mistaking it. He had a right to be upset, but there was another aspect. The fact was, he was also hurt. He considered our relationship to be of much greater value than to be treated so insensitively.

Criticism from a Loved One

Marriage is the most common arena for this type of spirited criticism. Someone has said, "You always hurt the one you love the most." "Why can't you be more considerate?" is a common criticism heard by thoughtless husbands. The reason a wife reacts that way is because she feels that if her husband loved her more, he would indeed be more considerate. To the husband it sounds awfully like a vicious attack, to which, as normal, he responds defensively. This, understandably, only adds fuel to the fire and a normally loving couple find themselves about to declare world war three! She did not start out rejecting him. Actually her criticism was really a cry from her heart saying, "Your inconsideration makes me feel like you are rejecting me."

It is plain to see that unless we learn to overcome the hurdle of criticism, life will inevitably become complicated. The following suggestions are offered with the hope that they will be as helpful to you as they have been to me.

First, we need to lift our hearts to the Lord and at the same time, count up to ten. Counting up to ten will help us not to make a hasty response and, at the same time, it provides a short space of time to listen in our hearts to anything the Lord may say. However, I need to warn you straight away that whenever I have done this, the Lord only ever points out where I have been in the wrong!

Second, when we welcome correction we are acting wisely. In Proverbs 13:1 we read, *"A wise son accepts his father's discipline."*

Third, *"Whoever loves discipline loves knowledge"* (Proverbs 12:1). The verse continues, *"But he who hates reproof is stupid."* Isn't that the truth!?

Fourth, just because your critic appears to have a bad attitude, don't allow yourself to be trapped into defensive behavior. First ask the question, "Is this true?"

Fifth, with the Lord's help, try to respond graciously together with a sense of dignity. Remember, *"A gentle answer turns away wrath"* (Proverbs 15:1).

Sixth, although this may seem to be near impossible, humble yourself and acknowledge when you have been in the wrong – the quicker the better. I referred earlier in this chapter to an elder who was expressing his pain and anger over the unilateral decision I had made. After he had been holding forth for a while about my behavior, I interjected with, "Tony (not his real name), you're right." I wasn't sure that he heard me the first time because he continued to go ahead at full steam, so again I spoke up, but this time a little more forcefully: "Tony, you are quite right. It was wrong of me to make that decision unilaterally. I'm sorry." This time he stopped in his tracks and I watched as all the anger drained from his eyes. That was the end of the matter. It finished right there and then.

Seventh, avoid making excuses and never ever respond by giving explanations as to why our critic is wrong. This behavior only serves to reveal our insecurity. When people respond defensively to our concerns, it has the effect of making us feel reluctant to try to help them on another occasion. I usually bring such conversations to a swift conclusion with, "You may well be right."

Criticism from My Enemy

Jesus continually suffered the unjust criticism of both the religious right – the "Pharisees" – and the religious left – the "Sadducees". They attacked Him for healing on the Sabbath; they questioned His ministry credentials because He allowed a prostitute to anoint His feet with precious oil and then wipe them with her hair. As if that wasn't bad enough, He then permitted her to repeatedly kiss the same feet and this was all going on whilst He was preaching! They said, *"If he was a prophet he would know what sort of woman she is."* On several occasions they complained scathingly that He was eating and drinking with sinners. He was constantly the object of their unrelenting disapproval.

So, how we conduct ourselves when faced with the same problems should be determined by the example Jesus set for us. Generally speaking, it seems that when Jesus was attacked, He responded with a lamb-like attitude. The most perfect example was the manner in which He allowed himself to be arrested and convicted on the basis of false evidence. When He went on the offensive however, His whole approach was quite different. He changed completely to become lion-like. On one memorable occasion recorded for us in Matthew chapter 23, He calls the Scribes and Pharisees "hypocrites, fools and blind guides", and if that wasn't enough, he referred to them as whitewashed tombs, beautiful on the outside but on the inside full of dead men's bones and all uncleanness! He completes His little homily by addressing them as "serpents" and, in particular, "a brood of vipers". Jesus obviously had never read the famous best-seller: *How to Win Friends and Influence People!* It seems that we so frequently act in the opposite way to Jesus. We are lion-like when we ought to be lamb-like and behave like wimps when we ought to be lion-like.

However, a word of caution might be called for lest we make the mistake of thinking we are equal with Jesus as far as our character is concerned. It is true that Jesus learned obedience through the things He suffered, but unlike us, there were no weak areas in His character. Therefore He could attack the Pharisees for their religious hypocrisy with integrity because He was completely clean from any such behavior Himself. The same cannot be said for ourselves. Another thing to bear in mind is this: sometimes those people who regard us as enemies and treat us as such may be some of the Lord's secret "disciplers". Their behavior has the excellent effect of driving us to our knees in desperation to plead for wisdom and strength and sometimes for vindication.

A pastor friend of mine was experiencing some severe resistance from a small number of disgruntled members in his congregation. They had a doctrinal difference with him and were quite upset about the direction he was taking the church. After a while they began to leave, one by one. On the morning he phoned me to say that the last one had left, he made a very interesting remark. He said, "Barney, instead of feeling relieved, I feel insecure. All the time that they were in the meetings, it had the effect of pushing me into God. Their presence also motivated me to make sure I was preaching sound doctrine; now that they have gone I no longer feel those same constraints."

Whenever we try to vindicate ourselves, it means we are doubting God's character. Our self-vindication implies that we think He will break His promise to bring forth our vindication.

In closing let me offer a few thoughts to those of us who from time to time take the liberty of handing out constructive criticism.

First, we need to be certain the Holy Spirit is leading us to offer our concerns to the unsuspecting recipient.

Second, we should ask ourselves: "Is this relationship strong enough to survive my critical advice?" I once heard it said, "You cannot drive a ten-ton lorry over a three-ton bridge."

Third, try to do it from a humble spirit, remembering it might be you who is on the receiving end next time round.

Fourth, do it by way of an appeal. Paul instructed Timothy in 1 Timothy 5:1 not to sharply rebuke an older man, but rather appeal to him as a father. He also advised him to approach the younger men as brothers, the older women as mothers, and the younger women as sisters. Sometimes it is better to bring a criticism on the basis of what you "feel" rather than what you "think". Rather than using phrases like, "You always do this . . . " or "You never . . . ", try saying, "I feel like you always . . . " and "It feels to me like you never . . . ". The latter approach has the effect of drawing out of the person a feeling of sadness or regret for their behavior, whereas the first approach only causes them to become defensive.

Fifth, share your concern privately. Some people seem to need a group setting in order to confront another, but that kind of confrontation is seldom appreciated. It's commonly called "A coward's castle."

Sixth, always communicate your concern in such a way that the other person believes you recognize the possibility that your perspective could be wrong.

Seventh, ask yourself, "Have I a right to criticize this person?" Parents, especially when their children are young, not only have a right to correct their children, it is their duty to do so. But as the children get older and approach their late teens, increasing care needs to be taken not to handle them as if they are still young children. I have had quite a number of adults tell me that they are reluctant to visit their parents simply because they never seem to receive any respect. They feel they are being kept in perpetual childhood.

Chapter 4

The Purpose of Pruning

"... and every branch that bears fruit,
He prunes it so that it may bear more fruit."
(John 15:2)

When addressing a group of leaders, I have frequently taken the
opportunity to ask the question, "Practically speaking, how does
God prune us?" On every occasion the responses received have
been what I term "religious" ones. Typical answers are, "The
Lord is teaching me patience" or "God is requiring me to spend
more time in prayer" etc. – all of which are worthy considera-
tions, but they miss the point.

Let's look at the text. The word "prune" means to "cut off" or
to "cut back". The reality is: when God prunes you there is a loss!

Jesus used the analogy of pruning a tree to show how God
works in a person's life to refine them. The branch in Jesus'
analogy had no doubt been doing something worthwhile – it was
a fruit-bearing branch. In other words, it had been a success. But
in spite of all that, along comes the farmer or one of his workers
and starts cutting off the very parts of the vine that had served
him so successfully. It doesn't make sense and it doesn't seem
fair. The fact is, the farmer knows that unless he carries out this
radical surgery, next year the fruit will be decidedly inferior and
not marketable.

Pruning tends to take place through the everyday circumstances of life and inevitably through our circle of relationships.
In church life, this pruning activity could mean the choir leader
or worship leader being asked to hand over their responsibilities
to another. The same could be true for house group leaders,
ushers, youth fellowship leaders; or it may mean simply a choir
member being told that his services are no longer required.

The story is told of a member of the choir of a black church in the southern state of Alabama. Aaron had recently joined the choir, but it was soon quite noticeable that he was not only unable to hold a note but, even worse, he was tone deaf. The choir master was extremely embarrassed. But having tried delicately to approach the matter with Aaron and having found him to be unresponsive, he decided to fix an appointment with the pastor and ask for his assistance. The pastor was most sympathetic. "Just leave it to me," he said, "I'll take care of it."

The following Sunday he caught Aaron as he was leaving the morning service and took him aside into his office. "I'm so glad I've managed to see you, Aaron. We have a vacancy on our roster of ushers and I couldn't help noticing your warm smile and approachability; so I have been wanting to ask you whether you would be so gracious as to become one of our ushers?" A disturbed frown came over Aaron's countenance. "Pastor," he said, "I don't want to be an usher. I wanna sing, I wanna sing." The pastor now put on his best look of sincerity, at the same time placing his hand on Aaron's shoulder. Looking straight into his eyes he responded: "But brother Aaron, there are lots of people who can sing in the choir; we need an usher." By now Aaron was getting rattled, "No, I'm sorry pastor, I wanna sing and that's that." The pastor now knew he had to talk straight: "Aaron," he said, "the fact is, you can't sing." "That's nothing," retorted Aaron, "people are going round saying you can't preach neither!"

Being pruned is never an enjoyable experience. There is frequently a sense of shame coupled with a feeling of failure. Sometimes the recipients of pruning see themselves as victims who are being unfairly treated.

The older a person is and the longer they have held a position of responsibility, the harder it is for them to relinquish their hold of that appointment. Take the case of seventy-five-year-old Miss Stock: she was a deaconess and the pianist at a little Baptist church where I also happened to be a deacon and where, from time to time, I deputized for her at the piano.

It came about, much to her chagrin, that the church purchased a new Compton electronic organ. The reason for her resistance to the purchase was that she knew that her services would no longer be required because she was unable to play an organ. The fact was, she wasn't doing too well at the piano either! On the other hand, I happened to be more suited to playing an organ than the piano. Everyone in the church loved the sound of the new organ and preferred to have me play it rather than endure the declining efforts of Miss Stock on the piano. Eventually, the whole matter was raised and discussed at the deacons' meeting resulting in poor Miss Stock being asked to resign. It was impossible not to notice her pain and disappointment as she struggled with the new reality. As we get older, it is important to recognize that this type of pruning will be inevitable.

The Secular, the Sacred and the Spiritual

Now Jesus is obviously speaking in John 15:2 about bearing spiritual fruit. However, the principle remains the same even in secular life. With God, there is no fundamental difference between the sacred and the secular. Simply put, they are two separate spheres of life, but both are alike to Him. The spiritual principle applies to each. God will use his pruning knife in the home and in the workplace just as much as in the church.

There are so many different ways and situations in our secular life in which God can prune us. To try and mention as many as possible would not be helpful to the purpose of this chapter. However, a few examples would serve our purpose.

First of all, let's take the matter of demotion. I don't know which is worse: being fired or being demoted. One person described their feeling of shame in this way: "I just didn't know how to keep my head up. I could tell everybody was feeling embarrassed. It was like dying a thousand deaths." Demotion carries with it such an intense feeling of shame. It is rare for someone in big business or the civil service to be demoted, but when it does happen, the management usually transfers the one demoted to another district, away from their former colleagues. In the armed forces, if the reason for demotion is a minor one, the authorities are more likely to actually promote the person and transfer him to an office administrative posting rather than dishonor him in front of his subordinates.

Almost every time a person is demoted it entails a reduction in wages, which also intensifies the feeling of being dishonored. This issue of financial dishonor is not insignificant; several times in the Scriptures the word "honor" actually refers to a person's wages. Take for instance 1 Timothy 5:17:

"The elders who rule well are to be considered worthy of double honor."

In the case of someone being fired, not only can there be feelings of shame, self-pity, failure and unfairness, but often an overwhelming sensation of fear and insecurity. Again, the older a person is, the greater these feelings are intensified. Some time ago, a forty-five-year-old close friend of mine, who held a senior position in a large multi-national company, was given the sack. I was staying at his house when he was given the news. He returned home that evening with an extremely heavy heart. Overnight he seemed to change into an old man. I knew he felt it keenly!

I interrupted the writing of this chapter to phone him and ask what he had really felt during the crisis. "It was worse than I had imagined," he said. "It was total devastation! I felt like I had died! It was unbelievable! It was an all-time low! It was like everyone wrote you off!" He went on to say how he had returned to his former place of employment to give back the company car. This was the place where a few days before he had been the manager. Having handed the car keys back, he waited for his wife to come and pick him up. It took over half an hour. During that time no one enquired how he was doing. In fact, whilst he waited for his wife not one person came up and talked to him. He said, "I felt like I had leprosy."

There is a happy ending to this story. My friend after five months' unemployment, found a new job with another multi-national company. His salary dropped by $25,000 initially, but within twelve months he was earning more than he was receiving in his former employment.

Sport is another area where participants can expect to be pruned. How about committees or politics? Wherever appointments are made through use of the democratic process, sooner or later one must expect to lose an election.

Lack of finance can be the reason why it is necessary to cut back on some cherished activity. Other reasons can be injury, ill health, old age, or new responsibilities.

Take, for instance, motherhood: Over the years and on numerous occasions, young mothers have complained to my wife, Janette, of having to stay at home with the children and missing out on all the fun. Janette always responds with the same advice. "Embrace it. This is a season in your life. It is a blessing from the Lord." Children are not given to us to be obstacles to our personal preferences: on the contrary, they are treasures to be invested in. That means we must make them a priority.

Steps That Will Ensure Fruitfulness

The first thing to recognize when being pruned is: it is our Heavenly Father who does the pruning. Jesus said in John 15:1:

> *"I am the true vine, and My Father is the vinedresser."*

If we lose sight of this truth, we cannot help but wrongly evaluate pruning experiences. Our heavenly Father only has our best interests at heart. So, whatever He does or permits to be done to us, we can be sure it is intended for our good and not for our ill. Having established that foundational fact, it is important to point out that God appraises everything in heaven and on earth in the light of eternity, whilst we earthlings tend to assess the events of life within the limits of time and space. God sees everything in the vastness of eternity and, in particular, He views us as being in His eternal Son. This is why the Bible says, *"we see through a glass, darkly"* (1 Corinthians 13:12 KJV).

Therefore, not all of His surgical procedures will necessarily be seen to produce fruit in our lifetime on earth; much of it will be storing up treasure in heaven. As Paul points out in 2 Corinthians 4:16–18:

> *"Therefore we do not lose heart, but though our outer man is decaying, yet our inner man is being renewed day by day. For momentary, light affliction is producing for us an eternal weight of glory far beyond all comparison, while we look not at the things which are seen, but at the things which are not seen; for the things which are seen are temporal, but the things which are not seen are eternal."*

I acknowledge that this is not the only aspect of fruitfulness, but it is nonetheless an important one. For instance, people who are only able to measure the negative sides of old age through time/space spectacles are left with the conclusion: "What good can come out of this?'' Whereas those who put on their sky-blue tinted, eternity glasses are able to see immeasurable tons of glorious, indestructible treasure. As William Cowper the hymn writer put it:

> ''Blind unbelief is sure to err,
> And span his work in vain;
> God is his own interpreter,
> And he will make it plain.''

The second thing to keep in mind is: this pruning experience will eventually bear fruit.

It is not possible to talk about God's pruning activities without thinking of Joni Eareckson Tada. She was a fine Christian teen-ager, but with little likelihood of ever making a national, spiritual impact in America. One day, she had the misfortune to hit her head on the hard floor of the ocean bottom. As a result, she suffered a broken neck which left her a quadriplegic, drastically cut back physically. Who amongst us would not find ourselves shaking our heads and saying, ''What a waste''? But we would be wrong, terribly wrong. As a result of this accident and most importantly, because of Joni's response to it, she has a ministry that reaches around the world. Her books have been translated into dozens of languages. This little insignificant nobody has touched millions of lives for eternity. Isn't that one of the most remarkable stories in the history of mankind?

Thirdly, our response to God's pruning will determine whether we will bear more fruit or whether we end up in the gall of bitterness. If we accept the sovereignty of God and believe that nothing happens to the child of God by mistake; if we can trust our heavenly Father that He means it for our good and not our ill; if we can forgive and bless all those who may have been the instruments God used to effect the pruning; if we can rest in the knowledge that God keeps His word and that this experience will eventually produce fruit; then fruitfulness is assured.

Fruitfulness

What about fruitfulness? What does it mean? Some will say it is the fruit of the Spirit – in other words godly character. My evangelist friends will immediately wave their flag to draw attention to the fruit that speaks of the harvesting of sinners into the kingdom and they would be equally right. We have already pointed out that some fruit will not be seen this side of heaven. But let me close this chapter by suggesting that there is a fruit more succulent, more deliciously sweet than all the others. It is a realm of fruitfulness that only God can fully appreciate. It is fruit that is specially reserved for the throne room of heaven. In all honesty, I don't think I have been able to bear much of this fruit yet, but there is a longing deep down inside that cries out to my God saying, "Lord I desire to be a branch that bears such fruit."

I cannot put it better than Madam Guyon in her lovely poem *Resignation*:

> A little bird I am,
>   Shut from the fields of air;
> And in my cage I sit and sing
>   To Him who placed me there;
> Well pleased a prisoner to be,
>   Because, my God, it pleases Thee.
>
> Naught have I else to do;
>   I sing the whole day long;
> And He whom most I love to please
>   Doth listen to my song;
> He caught and bound my wandering wing,
>   But still He bends to hear me sing.
>
> Thou hast an ear to hear,
>   A heart to love and bless;
> And though my notes were e'er so rude,
>   Thou wouldst not hear the less;
> Because Thou knowest, as they fall,
>   That love, sweet love, inspires them all.
>
> My cage confines me round;
>   Abroad I cannot fly;
> But though my wing is closely bound,
>   My heart's at liberty.
> My prison walls cannot control
>   The flight, the freedom, of the soul.

O, it is good to soar
    These bolts and bars above,
To Him whose purpose I adore,
    Whose providence I love;
And in Thy mighty will to find
    The joy, the freedom, of the mind.

           (Jenne Marie De La Motte-Guyon,
                1648–1717, tr. unknown)

Chapter 5

Handling Rejection

The first thing that caught my eye as I walked into our Sunday morning service was a visitor sitting three rows from the back. The woman was in her early forties, with unkempt, dyed, blond hair reaching to the shoulders. Her hair was showing at least two inches of dark at the roots. Her eyes were red and puffy and the tears that streamed down her face left behind dark traces of mascara. She looked a sorry sight. It was all too clear that life had not been kind to her. She continued to quietly weep throughout the whole service.

She had accepted an invitation to our morning meeting by one of our elderly couples on condition they completely safeguarded her anonymity. So, when I asked at the door as to who she was, they quickly replied on her behalf, "This is Beryl, a long-time friend." I could tell by the tone of voice and the look in their eyes that this was not the time to enquire further. Three days later I picked up the mail and found a letter with the words "Strictly Confidential", scrawled across the back. It was from Beryl. Could she see me urgently? She stated she was in a lot of trouble and was certain the police were looking for her!

She arrived early the next day for her appointment and was clearly nervous as she sat uneasily on the edge of the settee, clutching a handkerchief. Slowly Beryl told her story. "I'm a drug addict," she said, "I have been addicted to morphine for over eighteen years. It all started when I was a missionary in Africa. I had gone out as a nursing sister and had only served at the mission hospital for a few months when I discovered a white member of staff having an affair with one of the nationals. I discreetly approached the senior leader of the Mission and informed him of my discovery, but was told I had a bad attitude and a vivid imagination and needed to repent." Tears filled her eyes as she painfully recalled, "I was absolutely devastated."

She was immediately sent back to England, but inexplicably was allowed to return to the hospital six months later.

Shortly after her arrival she had an accident and suffered a broken arm. The fracture was so painful that morphine was prescribed. Beryl found it not only eased the pain, but it also gave her an intense feeling of warmth and pleasure. When the treatment finished, Beryl, who had the key to the medicine cupboard, began to secretly help herself to more morphine. She knew it was wrong, but she just couldn't help it. She was hooked!

It wasn't long before her sin was discovered and without any offer of help or guidance she found herself expelled from the Mission and back in Britain. The news spread fast amongst her friends as well as the members of her home church who had sent her out to Africa. As a result, she found it impossible to go back to them; the shame was too intense.

At the same time, Beryl discovered that she could satisfy her addiction by drinking a particular brand of cough mixture. She raised enough money by being a resident nurse and nanny to new-born babies. She figured that without having to have an employment card, she could evade paying taxes, so for eighteen long years she had lived in constant fear of being caught. Life had become a living hell. Like the prodigal son, she had finally come to an end of herself. It was either suicide or come clean. So it was that she found herself in our morning meeting and later in my home sharing her tragic story.

Getting her off and keeping her free of morphine was the easy part, but far more difficult was to see her healed from the painful memories and resentment she continued to retain towards the Missionary Society and, in particular, the Field Chairman. As a result Beryl had great difficulty with anyone who held a position of authority. For instance, on one occasion a church elder called at her house to enquire after her health as she had been absent for the previous two Sundays. To his utter astonishment, instead of receiving a warm welcome, she hit him! Wisely he beat a hasty retreat.

It took a long time before it finally dawned on us that there was a deeper underlying cause. Eventually, she fully opened her heart and told us, "I came from a broken home. After my father and mother split up, my mother took in a lodger but the truth was, they lived together as husband and wife. This made him my step-father. It seemed alright to start with, but after a while he began to be quite cruel towards me. I would watch enviously as he put his arm around my mother and then it became utterly unbearable when my little brother was born. He seemed to show so much affection to him, but not once did he ever say one kind word to me or touch me lovingly. All I ever received from him were angry tongue lashings, often accompanied by outbursts of violence. What made it worse was that my mother never once tried to protect or console me. Then came the incident that seemed to break my heart for ever. I was only six at the time and Christmas was only a few weeks away. I decided to save all my pennies and buy my step-father a special present. I would wrap it up in bright Christmas paper and on Christmas morning at the right moment, I would present it to him. I was absolutely certain that this would win his heart. I went to bed each night dreaming of what would happen: I could see the look of surprise that would spread across his face as I handed him his gift. I saw him reaching out his hands and gathering me into his big strong arms, putting me on his knee and cuddling me. At last I would really be his little girl. Finally, Christmas morning arrived; my present had been waiting, ready for days. He was sitting in his favorite armchair; now was the moment. I quickly retrieved the parcel from where it had been hidden and walked into the room. With eager anticipation I walked over to his chair, handed him the present and said, 'Happy Christmas, Daddy.' He looked at it for a moment, then at me, then scornfully tossed it into the corner of the room saying, 'I don't want your stupid present.' I was devastated. I thought my little heart would burst. Picking up the present I ran to my room and falling on my bed I sobbed and sobbed for hours. It was the worst Christmas of my life. From that day to this I've never trusted another man."

Now we understood! Beryl, at the tender age of six had been cruelly rejected. The effect on her was nothing less than disastrous. From then on, and throughout all the intervening years, she was constantly stumbling over this impossible hurdle.

There was a happy ending to this story. After careful and prayerful counsel Beryl eventually became completely free. She paid her tax arrears and her name was restored to the Royal College of Nurses membership list. She also obtained an excellent nursing appointment and held it until retirement. I'll explain later the steps she took that won back her freedom.

Examples from the Bible

There are a number of examples found for us in the Scriptures, the first one being the story of Cain and Abel. The Bible says in Genesis 4:5,

> *"but for Cain and for his offering He had no regard. So Cain became very angry and his countenance fell."*

Notice, it wasn't only the offering that was rejected, but Cain himself. The knowledge that both Abel and his sacrifice were accepted only served to aggravate Cain's intense feelings of rejection. The thought of it continually ate away at his insides. Eventually, it so turned his heart against his brother that, one day, whilst they were out in the field together and in the heat of the moment, as Genesis 4:8 records it, *"Cain rose up against Abel his brother and killed him."*

It started with rejection; it ended with murder.

Joseph, on the other hand, in spite of being cruelly rejected by his brothers, refused to allow the memory of their despicable behavior destroy him. In the end, when he had it in his power to exact revenge, God used him to be the provider of food in the time of famine. Unlike Cain, instead of killing them he ended up saving them.

Another example is the case of David who was rejected by King Saul. Like Joseph's brothers the root cause for rejection was jealousy. One day, Saul, who up until this moment in time had held David in high regard, heard the women who had gathered from all the cities of Israel dancing and singing, "Saul has slain his thousands and David his ten thousands." When Saul heard this he was so overwhelmed with jealousy and fear that he began to believe that David, because of his popularity, could end up taking the kingdom. From that day on he began to take steps to kill him and on one occasion actually attacked David with a javelin.

In Ezekiel chapter 3 we also read of the prophet Ezekiel being rejected. In verse 4 God says, *"Son of man, go to the house of Israel and speak with My words to them."* In verse 7 God informs him, *"yet the house of Israel will not be willing to listen to you."* This piece of information did not sit very well with the prophet as we learn in verse 14: *"So the Spirit lifted me up and took me away; and I went embittered in the rage of my spirit."*

Rejection is Powerful

Rejection seems to have such an intense impact on people's lives no matter what age they are. Jenny was only six years old when her father left home for another woman. I first met Jenny when she was thirty-five. She lay in bed paralyzed from the neck down. The doctor told me, "Basically there is nothing organically wrong with her; in the medical profession we describe this condition as hysteria. That is why I recommended that you be invited to see her." She told me that soon after her father left home, the woman who he went to live with gave birth to a baby boy. She said, "I absolutely hated that little boy." Her mother also helped in producing this state of hysteria. Every night when Jenny said her prayers, her mother taught her to pray, "And please God, punish Daddy." The thing that Jenny struggled with the most was the thought that her father had forsaken her and embraced his new baby son. She was rejected.

I have heard medical and social experts say, "Children are very resilient. They just bounce right back and get on with life." That may seem true on the outside, but it is definitely not so on the inside. Take, for instance, the story of Gary. For thirty-five years Gary had not even shed one tear. He regarded himself as somewhat of a failure and generally expected people to eventually reject him, which in some cases is exactly what happened. The day came when he decided to get some help, so he asked some other leaders and myself to pray with him about his problem. During our praying together we enquired into his childhood and he told us the following account:

> "I was about eight years old and the youngest boy out of eleven children; I was continually the odd one out. My next eldest brother had lots of friends and I longed to be included. I remember the many times I asked, 'Can I play with you?' and they would just laugh and say, 'You're too small,' and run off. One day, to my immense surprise and pleasure, they invited me to join them in playing hide-and-seek. They chose to hide and I was the one to find them. Not

for one moment did I suspect a wrong motive. I was to stand in the garden shed, close my eyes and count up to ten, then start looking for them. They all filed out of the shed and then to my absolute horror I heard the bolt on the outside of the door being drawn. Off they all ran; it was all a game at my expense. I was trapped! As I heard the sound of their voices grow fainter my heart began to pound with fear and panic gripped hold of me. I pressed the weight of my body against the door with all my strength but the door wouldn't budge. I began to cry out in sheer terror and eventually with blood pouring out of my fingertips I clawed my way out through a crack in the paneling. Since that day I have never shed another tear."

Gary in response to our counsel began to pray for his brother and his brother's friends, declaring forgiveness and asking for God to bless them. As he started to pray, tears flowed freely down his cheeks. The pathway to freedom at last, was beginning to open up. At the time of writing, Gary is still working through the areas that remain unresolved, but God is helping him and clear progress is being made.

A sixty-year-old lady came up to me after a Sunday morning service and told me she had been adopted immediately after she was born. She had never seen her natural parents, but always had a deep longing to meet them. During the previous twelve months she had been making enquiries through the Salvation Army who, to her great joy, discovered that her parents were still alive and were living in Wales. The Salvation Army furnished her with the address. With great excitement and not a little apprehension she wrote to them explaining that they were her father and mother and asking if it would be possible for her to visit them as she was longing to meet them. Choking back the tears she said to me, "Pastor, I got a reply from them yesterday, and do you know what? They don't want to see me." All I could do was hold her hand and weep with her. Sixty years of age and still rejected!

Effects of Rejection

There are three main effects on people who have been rejected. The first is: the person rejected feels devalued. I'm not a great believer in the current emphasis amongst evangelicals which encourages people to seek for self-esteem. Esteem is what others are supposed to give and we receive; it is not for us to grasp and take. At the same time I believe there is an intrinsic value set upon us by God who made men and women in His likeness. Therefore, it is a healthy exercise sometimes to sit down and contemplate on the truth that we are fearfully and wonderfully made and that we who were nobodies are now, through Christ's death and resurrection, the special people of God. There is every reason for believers to lift their heads up, pull their shoulders back and walk tall in the knowledge that they are a new creation in Christ. The key to self-worth is Christ's worth. He alone is worthy. By His indwelling presence, we very ordinary clay pots become *"crowns of beauty"* and *"royal diadems"* in the hands of the Lord.

Secondly, a rejected person feels they have nothing to offer. God is a worker and has put ability into everyone to make worthwhile contributions to benefit others. People need to know that their lives make a difference whether they are believers or not. The reason many elderly people get so depressed is that they don't feel needed any more.

When I was a young immature pastor, we had a little old lady in our congregation called Mrs Munday. She was a delightful character. She always had a ready smile and never ceased to be grateful even for the smallest kindness shown her. When she reached her ninety-fifth year, she left her flat and went to live with her seventy-year-old daughter. One day when doing a pastoral visit, I found her seated by the kitchen door, peeling potatoes. The first thought that came to my mind was, "What a way to treat your mother! She should be able to relax in a nice armchair and enjoy being waited on." I cringe when I look back at my youthful ignorance. Her daughter was doing the most helpful thing possible. She was allowing her mother's life to make a difference. To those who may be asking, "Did she reach her hundredth birthday?" The answer is "yes", thanks to a wise and thoughtful daughter.

Thirdly, a rejected person feels to a certain degree that they don't belong. God made us to be social beings. It was God who said in Genesis 2:18, *"It is not good for the man to be alone."*

It is "Father" who has placed in us the desire to belong to His other children. The body of Christ is essentially relational; that is why we read that we are being *"fitted"* together, *"built"* together (Ephesians 2:19) and *"knit"* together (Colossians 2:2), and in Psalm 68:6 it says, *"God makes a home for the lonely."*

It is bad enough when someone's act of labor or artistic talent is rejected, but when a child perceives through certain actions of its parents that he or she is an outcast, it is an attack against their total personhood. Their longing to be loved and included becomes a shattered dream.

Overcoming Rejection

How does someone overcome the pain and damage incurred by being a victim of rejection? The true and effective answer can only be found when we start with Jesus. All other answers appear to begin with the "rejecter", but the Bible always takes us to the Lord. In Psalm 27:10 we read,

> *"For my father and my mother have forsaken me,*
> *But the LORD will take me up."*

And again in Hebrews 13:5 it says,

> *". . . for He Himself has said, 'I WILL NEVER DESERT YOU, NOR WILL I EVER FORSAKE YOU.'"*

One of the most comforting truths we can embrace is the knowledge that we don't have a high priest representing us who doesn't understand our problems but, on the contrary, he has been deeply touched with the feelings of our infirmities. In Isaiah 53:3 we have recorded for us the awful indictment that stands against the whole of mankind: *"He was despised and forsaken of men."*

John reports in the first chapter of his Gospel and verse 11: *"He came to His own, and those who were His own did not receive Him."* The Jews actually preferred a convicted murderer called Barabbas rather than Jesus. But, as we all know, the most agonizing words that ever passed the lips of Jesus were,

> *"'ELOI, ELOI, LAMA SABACHTHANI?' which is translated, 'MY GOD, MY GOD, WHY HAVE YOU FORSAKEN ME?'"*   (Mark 15:34)

For three dreadful hours the whole land was covered with darkness as Jesus, because of our filthy, vile sin was cut off from that pure, sweet, unclouded fellowship He had always enjoyed throughout eternity with His Father. There is no mistaking it, He was rejected! This is why there is no one better to talk to than Jesus. In the famous hymn "What a friend we have in Jesus", the second verse says:

> "Do thy friends despise, forsake thee,
> Take it to the Lord in prayer,
> In his arms He'll take and shield thee;
> Thou wilt find a solace there."

I am convinced that all the psychological help in the world would be insufficient to fully heal a person suffering from rejection, unless in the first place that help starts with Jesus.

Rejection is one of the chief causes of being scandalized. In chapter 7 I will be dealing with the subject of being scandalized. In it I will try and deal with root causes and then in chapter 8 seek to provide a biblical answer.

Chapter 6

The Scars of Abuse

Abuse: "An established unjust or corrupt practice."
(*The Concise Oxford Dictionary*)

In recent years the word "abuse" has been used to describe all sorts of unacceptable behavior. People talk about having their time abused, their health abused, their privacy abused. All of these usages may be proper, but in this chapter I want to talk about three rather more serious expressions of abuse that leaves its victims with deep emotional wounds. Without radical spiritual "surgery" these people become permanent casualties.

In the autumn of 1993 I was preaching to a large church congregation in southern England. I was speaking on the verse from Ephesians 6:2: *"Honor your father and mother"* when suddenly, and to the utter amazement of the people present, a man in his late twenties stood up at the back of the building and cried out at the top of his voice, "But what about if you have been abused?" You could hear the sound of pain in his voice. His interruption in actual fact fitted perfectly into my message because my next point was to pose the question, "But how can I honor my parents if they have abused me?"

During the past three years I have had the privilege of praying for several thousand people who have carried acute emotional injuries from childhood. Almost every one of them would break down weeping. You may find as you read the rest of this chapter that memories come flooding back from your childhood, recollections of things said or done to you that have been too painful to even think about. Some of you, as a consequence, may think of yourselves in one or more of the following ways: dirty, cheap, hated, unwanted, unfit, worthless or useless. If you discover tears beginning to flow, don't try and hold them back; as soon as emotionally possible, open your heart up to Jesus and tell Him in detail all about it. Then I would suggest you go to an understanding pastor and ask him for help. You might like to suggest to him that he reads this chapter before talking with you further. May the Holy Spirit help you as you continue to read.

The first area I want to address is sexual abuse. Some years ago I was visiting a church in England when an eleven-year-old girl came up to me and asked, "Mr Coombs, is it true that if you cannot forgive someone, you cannot receive the Holy Spirit?" I thought for a moment and then replied, "That is indeed true, because the Bible says, 'He gives the Holy Spirit to those who obey Him' and not to forgive someone is to disobey the command of Jesus." Her eyes began to mist up and then she slowly turned and walked away. A little while later she returned with a young friend. It was easily apparent that she had been crying. "It's my Daddy," she said, "he's been doing bad things to me." By now her mother had joined us and was totally devastated by the news. Her father, who was not a Christian had attended the meeting and was sitting at the back of the hall. The pastor of the church carefully confronted him but was only met with a flat denial that he had ever molested his daughter. That night the mother and her daughter together with her younger daughter stayed at the pastor's home which was where I also was staying. After reporting the matter to the police, which by the way is mandatory (failure to do so is a crime), I spoke to the young girl. "Sweetheart," I said, "it is very important that you forgive your Daddy. If you don't it will leave you damaged for life." She was absolutely adamant, "I will never forgive him, never." She lowered her voice, "I hate him for what he did to me." I asked her whether she would be willing to let me pray to Jesus that He would bring about a change in her heart so that she would find it possible to forgive her father. "Alright, I'll let you." I could not help a little smile; she said it so matter-of-factly. The good news is: on the morning her father was sentenced to four years' imprisonment, she phoned him and said, "Daddy, I forgive you for what you did, but please don't tell Mummy I phoned." Her mother did not forgive him and their marriage ended in divorce. However, her father not only repented of his crime and made a full confession, he also committed his life to Christ and is now walking with the Lord.

Recently, I heard of a pastor who has been accused and charged by the police for raping his two daughters. They are now adults but they claim that when they were children he molested one of them over six hundred times and the other one over eight hundred times. They have said to a friend of mine that they want to make him pay for what he did. I have no doubt in my mind that if he has committed these dreadful crimes, then he should be punished, but what worries me equally as much, is the desire that these women have in their hearts to exact revenge. They may succeed in putting him behind bars for a very long time, but unless something changes in their hearts and they forgive him, they will continue to live with their torment until the day they die.

When Janette and I first arrived in Vancouver, back in March 1976, the news headlines were totally absorbed with the case of a twelve-year-old girl who had been kidnapped on her way to school. After six months without the discovery of one single clue, everyone presumed that she had been murdered and her body dumped. One day the police were called to a domestic fight between a couple who lived in the house next door to this missing girl. The husband had been drinking and after taking notes for their report, the police left. Not long after, they were recalled to the same address by the man's wife who made another formal complaint but, as was the case before, there was insufficient evidence to arrest him; in any case, he was apparently no longer on the premises. However, just as the officers were about to drive away, they noticed the man emerge from his garage. One of the officers got out of the police cruiser and, after repeating a warning to the man, was ready to leave again when he thought he heard the faint cry of a child coming from the back of the garage. When he looked there was no sign of anyone in the garage – only a cupboard standing against the back wall with its door open. Then he heard the sound again. This time it seemed to come from the open door of the cupboard. He raced into the garage and looked into the cupboard. There he discovered a hole in the floor that opened up into an underground room. Through the dim light he was able to make out the emaciated form of the missing child. Her gaunt face and sunken eyes looked up appealingly as she feebly whispered, "Please help me." She couldn't even muster enough strength to climb the ladder. He reached down, gathered her up in his big strong arms and lifted her to safety. You can guarantee he will never forget that moment for the rest of his life.

Down below the stench was overwhelming, but this poor little child had been imprisoned there for over six months. He had kept her chained to a bed for much of the time. She lived off tinned food and water; her toilet was a bucket that remained unemptied for several days at a time. On two occasions he went away on holiday. One of these was for two weeks during which time she passed her twelfth birthday. News reporters wept openly when they examined her underground prison. They could only imagine what sadistic pleasure he had extracted at the expense of this pitiful, innocent youngster.

Later, when asked whether she had lost hope she replied, "Never! I kept praying to God every day and I knew He was going to help me get out." Then she made this astounding statement, "I have forgiven him, but I think he should be executed for what he did to me." As a matter of fact that is exactly the sentiments of Jesus. He put it like this in Matthew 18:6:

> *"but whoever causes one of these little ones who believe in Me to stumble, it would be better for him to have a heavy millstone hung around his neck, and to be drowned in the depth of the sea."*

There are many wives who feel sexually abused by their husband's excessive or unusual demands. I'm not easily shocked, but one evening I was confronted with a question from a married woman in a hotel lobby that I know caused my cheeks to blush. I had enjoyed a nice meal with a group of Christian leaders when one of the men present needed to go to his hotel room. As we walked through the hotel lobby on our way to the lounge his wife stopped me and said, "May I ask you a sensitive question?" I found myself just a little bit on my guard by the use of the word "sensitive" but didn't want to appear indifferent, so I quickly responded, "Sure, fire away." I'm sure her question made my mouth drop open. "What do you think about oral sex?" she asked, "Is it a sin or not?" After I had recovered my composure, I responded, "Lady, it would be wrong for me to reply without your husband being present." The next day, the pair of them came to see me. It was clear after talking with them that the wife was no religious prig; her problem was that she felt violated by some of her husband's fantasy adventures that left her feeling an object of lust rather than a sweetheart to be loved, caressed and enjoyed. It is not my desire to pass judgment on the subject of oral sex, other than to say that whatever takes place between a husband and wife whilst making love, needs to be mutually acceptable and enjoyed with a clear conscience.

Words Can Be Destructive Weapons

Solomon speaking about the tongue in Proverbs 15:4 says, *"perversion in it crushes the spirit"* and in Proverbs 12:18 we read, *"There is one who speaks rashly like the thrusts of a sword."*

I have seen men cry like babies as they have recalled the verbal abuse they received from their fathers. Some of these attacks actually amount to curses. One remembered his father saying in a fit of temper, "Damn you, boy, get out of my sight and never come back." One mother railed at her grown-up son, "If I never saw you again, nothing would make me happier." But some of these injurious remarks don't necessarily come out in temper tantrums; sometimes they can be far more damaging simply because they are spoken in such a measured way.

Take, for instance, Edward. At the end of the school year he had achieved straight "A"s in all his subjects; all that is, except one in which he managed a creditable "B". He brought his report card home and handed it to his father and stood by his chair waiting with eager anticipation. He looked for the smile of approval that he was sure would soon spread over his father's face, but it never came. Instead, his father tossed the report back to him and remarked, "How come you only got a 'B' for history, son?" A sword struck into his soul that day that thirty years later still had the powerful effect of reducing that man to weep uncontrollably. "Do you know what, Barney?" he once said to me, "I could never do enough to please him. I always was made to feel a failure."

One of the little pieces of advice I always give to intended bridegrooms is, "Be careful not to make stupid remarks to your wife on your honeymoon." In one marriage crisis in which I was asked to help, all went wrong on the couple's honeymoon. What was expected to be the next best thing to being in paradise was plunged into a most awful nightmare through one foolish comment by the husband. On the second day they happened to have a minor tiff which would have all been over in a minute if he hadn't made the explosive comment, "I think I have made an awful mistake." She quickly picked up on his words by asking, "What are you talking about? What awful mistake?" "Getting married to you, that's what I mean." She was devastated; she never recovered. I tried my best to bring about a reconciliation but all she could say was, "He says it was a mistake." They are now divorced!

It is not only men who verbally abuse their wives and children. On many occasions I have seen women verbally abuse their husbands. It may be true that women are the weaker vessel when it comes to physical strength, but it is certainly not the case when it comes to the use of the tongue. Proverbs 27:15–16 says,

> *"A constant dripping on a day of steady rain*
> *And a contentious woman are alike;*
> *He who would restrain her restrains the wind,*
> *And grasps oil with his right hand."*

In other words she is like a verbal juggernaut! Nothing can stop her.

A woman who openly expresses contempt for her husband is abusing him. If she constantly pulls him down with harping criticism, that also amounts to abuse.

There is however, one aspect of married life that requires special understanding and tenderness. Over the years I have been frequently sought out to give advice to husbands whose wives seem to have a difficult time during their menstrual period. Sometimes statements are made containing absolutes such as "you never" and "you're always" which serve to drive the husband into defensive mode and almost always end up in the couple having a row. These times usually only last for three or four days, but when a wife is in her late forties and early fifties things can be drastically worse. It is during these years that she will encounter the menopause. For the husband it is a time of confusion. His wife who is also his best friend, who most of the time would only speak and behave with thoughtfulness and tenderness, suddenly and without warning undergoes a pro-found personality change. He finds himself in a powerless and helpless place. Overnight she begins to treat him as if he is her worst enemy. Once they were sweethearts; now they are adver-saries. Nothing he says seems to make any difference. In these situations husbands need to know that in most cases, their wives' illogical behavior has very little to do with him, even though some of her verbal attacks may have a measure of substance to them. The fact is, she is going through a severe chemical and biological change in her female metabolism and this requires special understanding on his part. No matter how much her self-induced turbulence intensifies, he must remain like the Rock of Gibraltar. He must be firm but tender; give more cuddles not less; share more words of affection and appreciation not fewer. If he holds steady through the storm, they will come out the other side with greater commitment and be more "in love" than ever before. The sad thing is many husbands do not comprehend what is going on and overreact to their wife's behavior, even to the point of resorting to physical attacks – which brings me to the third aspect of abuse: the use of violence.

The Use of Violence is Limited to Lawful Government

As far as children are concerned, the Bible makes it abundantly clear that corporal punishment which comes from a parent's loving heart is not only permissible but is, indeed, advisable. Proverbs 13:24 says,

> *"He who withholds his rod hates his son,*
> *But he who loves him disciplines him diligently."*

Unfortunately, in our generation we are seeing a steady decline in the proper disciplining of children. As a result, children's behavior is becoming more rebellious and disobedient. Kids show little respect to adults; they are not taught to be grateful; sexual promiscuity is becoming increasingly prevalent amongst young teenagers. It is no small wonder that when parents do finally break down and use the rod, they tend to lose all self-control and end up by abusing their child instead of giving them loving correction. When the discipline is given out of love for the child, the child is left with memories of being loved instead of planting seeds of resentment.

When our daughter Rachel was about three years old, it was my turn to be looking after her, but I needed to go on some errands so I took her with me in the car. One of the places I had to call into was our local Christian bookshop. Because I was only going to be a few minutes, I left Rachel in the car. On my return I couldn't help but notice that her cheeks were bulging out on both sides and that brown colored saliva was dribbling out of the corners of her mouth. She had stuffed as many of my toffees into her mouth as possible and then with wide-eyed innocence had the cheek to say, "I haven't been eating your toffees, Daddy!" When we got home I carefully explained to her that, whilst she had been naughty to take Daddy's toffees without permission, she had been even more naughty to have told Daddy a deliberate lie, and for that she was to have a spanking, which she duly received. After her tears subsided, I continued to cuddle her and then made it clear to her that at no time had I stopped loving her. For several years after that episode she would clamber up on my knee and say, "It's true, isn't it Daddy. Even when I'm naughty you still love me." The interesting thing is, Rachel is now a married woman with children of her own, but every now and again she will say, "Dad, tell them about the time I took your sweets." That loving correction has become a treasured memory!

When I was a child my best friends, Tommy and Bobby, lived just a few houses away. Much of our free time was spent playing together. Many times during those early years when I called at their house to see if they wanted to come out to play, they would answer the door showing physical evidence that they had been beaten about by either their mother or their father. I have stood outside their kitchen window and heard their screams as their parents laid into them, kicking and punching them. These beatings often left them with nosebleeds and bruises. They weren't spanked – they were abused! They were terrified of their parents; for that matter, so was I!

I have listened to many stories by people who were violently abused by their parents. One man shared how he was chased by his drunken father who was armed with an axe. He could not remember how many times his father, under the influence of drink, waded into him with both fists. Two sisters told me all they could ever remember of both their parents was the sight of their clenched fists. They could never recall either parent ever reaching out with a hand of affection or sympathy.

Other Forms of Abuse

Before concluding this chapter there is one other form of abuse that is worth mentioning briefly, under the heading of "Mental

Cruelty". One young woman told me that as a child she absolutely hated wearing her long hair braided into plaits. One day, without her mother's permission, she stole into the bathroom with a pair of scissors and managed to cut off one of the plaits before her mother found her. Her mother was outraged and shouted, "You are going to pay for this my girl" and pay for it she did; the next day her mother forced her to go to school with just the one plait. The poor child was completely humiliated. That was, without doubt, mental abuse!

Another man told me that his parent's first child was "still born". The baby was a girl, which was all his mother ever wanted. So, when some years later he was born, his mother became bitterly disappointed and repeatedly told him so: "I never wanted a boy, I only ever wanted a girl." Worse than that, she forced him to wear girls' clothes right up until the age of five. This type of parental behavior is more common than most of us realize: boys dressed like girls, girls dressed like boys. It is no small wonder that these children end up experiencing an identity crisis by the time they reach their teens.

Some of these occurrences to which I have referred, especially those that happened during childhood, may need the sort of ongoing help that most pastors through time restrictions are not able to give.

Although many of us leaders have some serious misgivings about a lot of so-called Christian counseling, I am bound to say that there are now available some wonderful biblically-based Christian counselors who are able to provide the type of ministry that truly sets captives free.

If you have been stirred by what you have just read, take the opportunity of going first of all to Jesus and sharing it all with Him; after all, it's not for nothing that He is called the "Wonderful Counselor". After praying about it, you may still want to seek for help from your pastor. However, if you don't feel secure in going to him or her, I suggest you get in touch with a well-known, reputable Christian leader and see if they can recommend a suitable Christian counselor who may be able to help you further.

Chapter 7

The Test of Skandalon

Looking at this chapter heading, you may find yourself scratching your head and asking, "What on earth does the word 'skandalon' mean?"

Some years ago I heard Bob Mumford, a well-known American Bible teacher, preach a sermon using the word "skandalon" as the central theme of his message. Bob's organization is called "Life Changers" which, not only aptly describes his ministry, but also the next three chapters of this book. In fact, for some these chapters might better be called "Life Savers".

We all understand how necessary it is for a surgeon to make an incision in order to open up and uncover the parts of the body that require surgery. In the same way the previous chapters were designed to bring into the open those parts of our personality that were injured in the past and have remain damaged over the ensuing years. We are about to come to the heart of all I have been endeavoring to communicate: this is the moment of reckoning. We have cut through the outer layers; now we come to the vital parts!

The term *skandalon* is a New Testament Greek word meaning "stumble" or "offend". When we English-speaking people use the word "offend", it usually carries the sense of being annoyed, or feeling a bit upset. In some instances it may even be used to describe someone taking serious umbrage or momentary outrage. But very rarely would the word be used to portray long-term anger and permanent severance of a relationship. However, the Bible uses the word far more seriously. The word is probably better translated "scandalized" and conveys the concept of being trapped, similar to a bird being caught in a snare.

Up until modern times hunters would capture birds by propping up a net with a single stick. Attached to the bottom of the stick would be an enticing piece of food which birds would find irresistible. As soon as the bird took the bait the stick, which the Greeks called a "skandalon", would collapse to the ground trapping the bird under the net.

Being scandalized is an exceedingly serious matter as we are about to see. Remember, the words "offend", "stumble" and "scandalized" all come from the word *skandalon*.

Trapped Like a Bird

As we have already pointed out, a person who has become scandalized is like a bird trapped in a net. It happens to be extremely difficult for them to escape. In Proverbs 18:19 we read, *"A brother offended is harder to be won than taking a strong city."*

There are numerous churches around the world that have Christians on their membership lists who, in years gone by, took offence with one another and subsequently have doggedly refused to be reconciled. It is a blight on the church and a major hindrance to God's blessing. They sit at the same communion table receiving the same bread and wine; they can be heard singing with much sincerity the great songs of the church, even,

> "Blessed be the tie that binds
> Our hearts in Christian love,
> The fellowship of kindred minds
> Is like to that above."

Yet, come the end of the service, they will walk out of the building in the same manner as they have every week, always making sure they carefully avoid one another. If it happens to be the minister with whom they are offended, then they either stop attending the services or they slip outside during the singing of the final hymn, thus avoiding the shaking of hands. What a sad state of affairs!

Opportunities to Be Scandalized Are Inevitable

I was playing snakes and ladders with my grandchildren during the Christmas holidays and couldn't help noticing that there were more snakes on the board than there were ladders. Who-ever designed the game, made sure it would be almost impossible to travel from the bottom to the top without landing on a snake's tail and encountering the big slide. However, I suppose there is a faint chance one could achieve the impossible, but not so in real life. Jesus said, in Matthew 18:7, *"It is inevitable that stumbling blocks come."*

Life is full of opportunities for offence: a birthday forgotten, a wedding invitation declined, an accident in the car, a joke in poor taste, double-booking an appointment . . . I could go on and on. Take, for instance, the case of a phone call not returned. Tim was a young pastor with whom I had been fairly close for a number of years; in fact, in some ways he received me as a mentor and spiritual father. It came about that we needed to do some serious talking together in matters pertaining to church and marriage. I wrote to him beforehand spelling out my concerns so that when we met, the things I had to say, would not come as a complete surprise.

We lived about two thousand miles apart so we fixed a date when I would be preaching in a city closer to his home, after which we would both fly to a city somewhere in the middle and have our little chat. I actually traveled four hours by car the previous evening and stayed overnight in a hotel in order to catch the early morning flight. I had inadvertently failed to ascertain the name of the airline, the flight number and time of his arrival so, just before I left for the airport, I phoned his home in order to get the information. His wife answered the phone and after exchanging a few pleasantries I asked if I could speak to Timothy. "I'm afraid he's in the shower," she replied. "That's alright," I said, "you can let me know what flight he's on and what time he's arriving." "Barney, I don't understand what you are talking about," she said, "Tim's not going anywhere today." Eventually, Tim came to the phone and confirmed what his wife had said. So I asked him, "Why aren't you coming?" He responded, "Because you have failed to return my phone calls at least six times during the past twelve months." I was dumbfounded; I could not believe what I was hearing. "But Tim," I protested, "do you mean to say that you were just going to let me travel a thousand miles to meet you and then leave me there at the airport to wait for you to show up?" "Yep, that's the way it is. I thought it was time you got some of your own medicine."

Of course, I was wrong not to have returned his calls. I couldn't remember the occasions he referred to, neither was it done deliberately. But the fact is, opportunities to be scandalized are to be found every day of our lives.

The Closer the Relationship, the Deeper the Wound

It seems providential that Janette and I were listening today to a splendid performance by Kathleen Battle and Jessye Norman. They were singing an old negro song about being scandalized. It went like this:

> [Kathleen]:
> *Well, I met my sister the other day*
> *I gave her my right hand*
> *Just as soon as my back was turned*
> *She scandalized my name*
>
> [Jessye]:
> *Well, I met my neighbor the other day*
> *I gave her my right hand*
> *Just as soon as my back was turned*
> *She scandalized my name*
>
> [Kathleen]:
> *Well, I met the deacon the other day*
> *I gave him my right hand*
> *Just as soon as my back was turned*
> *He scandalized my name*
>
> [Jessye]:
> *Well, I met the preacher the other day*
> *I gave him my right hand*
> *Just as soon as my back was turned*
> *He scandalized my name*

The song ends with the rhetorical question:

> Do you call that a sister? No, no.
> Do you call that a neighbor? No, no.
> Do you call that a deacon? No, no.
> Do you call that a preacher? No, no.
> Do you call that religion? No, no.
> No! No! No!

If we were to take a poll amongst scandalized people we would find the person most likely to be involved in offending them was a close relative such as father, mother, wife, husband, brother, sister and, in the case of sexual abuse, a grandfather or an uncle.

False Expectations

Part of the root cause of people becoming scandalized is "false expectation" or "unrealized expectation". For instance, Cain expected God to receive his offering. When God refused his sacrifice and he observed that Abel's sacrifice was received, he became deeply offended and, as a result, he ended up murdering his brother.

Sarah expected to have a baby, but when she still remained barren she encouraged her husband to commit adultery. Esau, although he had sold his birthright to his brother Jacob, still expected the birthright blessing. When he discovered that Jacob had got there first, his heart was filled with murderous intent. Hannah was desperate to have a baby. No doubt the bitter provocation by Peninnah, Elkanah's other wife, did not help matters; nonetheless Hannah expected God to give her a child. Eli discovers her in the temple praying, weeping "bitterly" for a baby.

The Bible records that Naaman was the captain of the King of Syria's army; that he was a great man, a highly respected and valiant warrior. He also had leprosy – a most serious, infectious disease that left its victims deformed, disfigured and social outcasts. His wife's maid, who had been kidnapped from Israel, learned of Naaman's condition and suggested that he visit the prophet Elisha who, at the time, was living in Samaria. She was certain that he would be able to cure the leprosy. Eventually, Naaman turned up outside Elisha's house accompanied by his entourage of horses and chariots. To the captain's utter disgust, Elisha didn't even come out to greet him. He simply sent his servant out with the message:

> *"Go and wash in the Jordan seven times, and your flesh will be restored to you and you will be clean."* (2 Kings 5:10)

The Bible goes on to say in verse 11 that Naaman became absolutely furious and went away and said:

"Behold, I thought: 'He will surely come out to me and stand and call on the name of the LORD his God, and wave his hand over the place and cure the leper.'"

Naaman had false expectations of how Elisha would handle the situation and, unless his servants had managed to persuade him to do as the prophet had instructed, he would have returned home still a leper. He nearly missed his healing!

Finally, Jonah expected God to destroy Nineveh, but when God failed to carry out the sentence which he had instructed the prophet to pronounce over the city, Jonah became so depressed he seriously contemplated committing suicide.

There are at least seven other reasons why people become scandalized; obviously there are more than seven, but these are the ones that stand out to me. Some of these have already been referred to earlier, in which case we will just make a passing comment and then move on.

First, the fall of a leader can have devastating repercussions. In the political scene governments have collapsed. In the religious domain congregations have been decimated due to the moral failure of their pastor. One church in the British Isles which, at one time numbered twelve hundred, was reduced in a matter of weeks to sixty five. Another church of fifteen hundred members was cut down to three hundred. In Zechariah 13:7 we read that when the shepherd is struck down, the sheep inevitably scatter. This is why Satan focuses a lot of his attention on Christian leaders.

Children are particularly affected when one of their parents departs from the straight and narrow. It is much, much worse if their parent is arrested for a sexual crime. I know how it affects them. On more than one occasion I have had the sad responsibility of trying to lift their heads up above their desolate shame and sense of betrayal.

Second, there is the offence which comes when calamity strikes. Some years ago in Northern California, due to unusual torrential rains, disastrous landslides were taking place with tragic results. In one such case a man, whose wife and two young children had perished, was being interviewed on the six o'clock prime time news. One could not fail to be moved as he described the depth of his emotions when he first discovered they were dead. But I will never forget his final words: "Now I know there isn't a God."

Third, the case of unrequited love or, worse still, a broken engagement. I have met the victims of such treatment wherever I have traveled, especially on the mission field. It is usually the women who are on the receiving end. Many of them never recover from the humiliation.

Fourth, having one's prayers unanswered. Andrea is an attractive thirty-five-year-old. She has a warm personality, a winning smile and a responsible position in the business she works for, but no husband. "I'm not the nice Christian you think I am," she confessed through her tears. "I feel very bitter towards God. It's not that men have not invited me out; the problem is, none of them are Christians." I couldn't promise her a husband but it was easy to understand her feelings. She prayed every day that God would bring the right man into her life but all to no avail.

John unexpectedly found himself out of a job. The government provided the usual unemployment benefit but this hardly covered the mortgage repayments. One of his children required orthodontic work, the cost of which was not covered by the National Health. He had also run up some heavy debts on his charge cards and, to make matters worse, he wasn't able to realize any equity in his house because there was none due to the economic recession. It was now worth less than the price he originally paid. He had heard all the great sermons, plus illustrations on God being Jehovah Jireh but where was God now when he needed Him the most? "I feel like throwing in the towel," he said. "What's the use of prayer, anyway?"

Fifth, being the victim of sexual abuse. I don't think I have ever heard anyone, no matter how long ago it happened, who doesn't break down in tears when they start to recount the story of how they were abused.

Sixth, children who are abused by their parents, either sexually, violently, or verbally. This type of abuse is probably the worst, simply because our parents are supposed to love and protect us. They are the ones we run to when we are in trouble. To whom can we run? It's an abuse of trust.

Seventh, carrying the offence of another. This is particularly dangerous when the victim happens to be a close relative or someone you love dearly. Proverbs 26:17 tells us:

> *"Like one who takes a dog by the ears*
> *Is he who passes by and meddles with strife not belonging to*
> *him."*

It seems that little grace is provided by God for those who find themselves getting embroiled in someone else's offence. It is also interesting to notice that those who can already be counted among the ranks of the scandalized, automatically gravitate towards those who are still in the early stages of being scandalized. The involvement of these veterans makes it much more difficult for the new casualty to accept the sort of radical surgery that is required; the advice that both sides will be offering is almost certainly going to be diametrically opposite to each other.

Chapter 8

Symptoms of Skandalon

Some people, having read thus far, may be asking the question, "How do I know whether I am indeed, scandalized?" Some may be wondering whether this is just a temporary upset that will go away of its own accord, the same way a common cold works its way through and out of the body.

If we have any one of the following symptoms it is almost certain we are already scandalized, or we are in the process of slowly succumbing to the disease.

The Film Keeps Running

The first symptom I have called the "Loop Film" syndrome. This is the person who having been offended, finds they are constantly rehearsing in their mind the details of what happened. Let's take the fictional story of Maureen, the mother-in-law of Daphne who has three young children, all under the age of five. Daphne and Frank (Maureen's son) live within a five-minute walk of Maureen, so she is easily available to baby-sit when Frank and Daphne want an evening out. Daphne and Frank are always struggling financially; whereas Maureen is well off and is very generous with gifts of clothing for the children as well as furniture for the children's bedrooms. In fact there is hardly a day Maureen doesn't pop round to see that everything is alright. However, all is not well. Daphne increasingly feels overwhelmed by her mother-in-law's constant presence together with all the gifts she showers upon the children and begins to complain about it to Frank. Eventually, after a few arguments between them both, Frank takes the opportunity to confront his mother the next time she visits the home. He tells her she is to stop coming round so frequently; she is to stop buying so many presents for the children and to make sure she recognizes Daphne as the children's mother and stop interfering when Daphne corrects the children. Maureen is thoroughly crushed and rushes out of the house in tears. That night she doesn't sleep a wink; she tosses and turns the whole night through. She hears the town clock strike on the hour and every half hour. All she can do is think about the unkind, ungrateful attitude of her son and his wife. She is convinced that this is all the work of Daphne and spends several hours making a mental list of all the nice gifts she has given her daughter-in-law; not to mention the countless times she has immediately dropped what she was doing and hurried round to Daphne's because of some urgent need. Maureen eventually falls asleep. After a few hours she wakes up. Her first thoughts are about yesterday's events. She thinks about it: at breakfast – in the shower – reading her Bible – trying to pray – driving the car; she just cannot break free from it. Sometimes she cries. Other times she imagines herself giving them a real piece of her mind. Many of her thoughts are irrational and in some moments of extreme emotion, Maureen may even consider suicide as a means of punishing them. In the same way that a loop film continuously plays the same action over and over, so Maureen finds herself helplessly trapped into repeatedly thinking through all her negative, painful memories relating to Frank and Daphne. It will be a long while before she remembers any of the good times.

The Tongue Keeps Talking

Symptom number two is the inability that Maureen has to refrain from talking about her offence to others. First of all she tells her pastor; she tells her house-group leaders, Roger and Joyce; in fact she makes an excuse to phone Joyce nearly every day in the hope that the conversation will turn towards her problem with Frank and Daphne. Then there is the weekly house group meeting where Roger asks the usual question: "Are there any matters for prayer this week?" Maureen cannot resist taking advantage of this opportunity. Even though the members of the group outwardly express their concern and sympathy, inwardly they grow increasingly worried for Maureen's mental and emotional state of health.

Some years ago, I knew a small group of leaders who used to meet every six months for mutual encouragement and an exchange of ideas. One of their number happened to become deeply offended with a close colleague of his. Every time the group met, it didn't take long before he would start to complain or give yet another example that had come to light about his friend's behavior. It finally came to the point where he was told that the next time they met, under no circumstances did they want to hear another word about his problem. They might have saved their breath; it was to no avail because he found it impossible to restrain himself. Talking about the offence becomes compulsive behavior. It is similar to an addiction. What controls our inward thoughts will dictate what comes out of our mouths. Jesus said so in Matthew 12:34:

"For the mouth speaks out of that which fills the heart."

Criticism Takes Over

The third symptom is a critical spirit. This is a more serious matter because it signifies that the offended person has now graduated from a conscious offence relating to one single matter to a subconscious state of mind that now distorts their whole view of life. They start to see something wrong with just about everything. The cup is half empty instead of being half full. There is always something wrong with the weather; either it is too hot or too cold; either there is too much rain or not enough. The preacher is too loud or too soft; too deep or too shallow and usually too long. The politicians are all out for their own interests and the neighbors are too nosey; their children are too noisy and their cat keeps doing its business in the garden. Once again the principle of *"what fills the heart controls the tongue"* is clearly evident; everyone and everything is spoken of negatively.

Such people become "party poopers" and what the Bible calls "murmurers" which in God's eyes amounts to very serious sin. All murmuring is ultimately a complaint against God's character and righteousness. Thomas Brooks describes murmuring as a "mother sin" because it gives birth to so many other transgressions.

In *The Works of Thomas Brooks* (Banner of Truth) he gives twelve reasons why it is profoundly wrong for believers to murmur. The following is one of them:

"The eleventh reason why Christians of all people would have least cause to be murmuring and muttering under any dispensation that we meet with in this world is this: Is not God your portion? Is not Christ your treasure? Is not heaven your inheritance? And will you murmur? Has not God given you a changed heart, a renewed nature and a sanctified soul; and will you murmur? Has he not given you himself to satisfy you, his Son to save you, his Spirit to lead you, his grace to adorn you, his covenant to assure you, his mercy to pardon you, his righteousness to clothe you; and will you murmur? Has he not made you a friend, a son, a brother, a bride, an heir; and will you murmur? Has not God often turned your water into wine, your brass into silver, and your silver into gold; and will you murmur? When you were dead did he not make you alive, and when you were lost did he not seek you, and when you were wounded did he not bind up your wound, and when you were falling did he not support you, and when you were down did he not raise you, and when you were staggering, did he not establish you, and when you were erring, did he not reduce you, and when you were tempted, did he not succor you, and when you were in dangers, did he not deliver you; and will you murmur? What! You are so highly advanced and exalted above many thousands in the world? Murmuring is a black garment, and it does not properly become the saints."

Murmuring is a symptom of an advanced state of being scandalized!

The Avoidance Game

Symptom number four is the inability to face the person who caused the offence. In many people it becomes a driving compulsion. They will go to what seems ridiculous lengths and almost any cost in order to avoid the meeting of faces. Take the story of John and Tracy who were struggling to lead their home fellowship. During a leaders' meeting, Judy, who together with her husband Doug, led another home fellowship, criticized John for the poor job he was doing with his group. Tracy was livid! "That's it," she said, "I will never speak to that woman again" and immediately set about keeping her word with a vengeance.

Where she and John sat in the Sunday morning service was determined by where Doug and Judy sat. Usually she liked to sit at the back, from where if necessary, she could make a quick exit. The Sundays that were Doug and Judy's turn to help serve the bread and wine at communion were particularly troublesome for Tracy. Her answer to the problem was to refuse to attend. Of course, she also insisted that she and John came off the communion serving rota. She was determined to do whatever was necessary to ensure she and Judy did not have to speak to each other.

I know of situations where offended people have locked themselves in their bedrooms, or hidden themselves in the bathroom, garage or garden shed, all for the purpose of avoiding meeting their adversary.

Forgiveness Is Not an Option

Symptom number five is the absolute inability to forgive the one offending, no matter what the Bible, and in particular Jesus, has to say about it. It seems impossible to penetrate their minds with the truth. They may say, "Yes, I know what you are saying is right, but I just can't bring myself to do it."

I have a friend who I love dearly, who has been deeply offended for years. I have pleaded with him time and again to extend forgiveness, but the hurdle is insurmountable. Even though the person who caused his offence has written to apologize and to ask for forgiveness, he still cannot bring himself to do it. A year ago I suggested that it was not necessary for him to personally meet up with his adversary – all he had to do was to write a short letter explaining that he was still struggling with what happened, but in obedience to Jesus and out of God's grace he was willing to forgive. My friend immediately responded positively to the idea, but I know as yet, nothing has happened. He's trapped! As mentioned already in this book: *"A brother offended is harder to be won than a strong city"* (Proverbs 18:19).

The challenge to forgive is typified in the unpronounceable Eskimo word, *Issumagijoujungnainermik*. When the Moravian Missionaries in 1764 went to preach the gospel to the Eskimos, they discovered that there was no word in the Eskimo language for forgiveness, so they invented the above word which means: "Not-being-able-to-think-about-it-anymore."

It is not only an individual who can find themselves scandalized. It can be true for a nation. For instance, I have yet to meet a non-Christian Jew who will forgive the Germans for the Holocaust. The standard reply when I have asked if they would forgive the German people for what happened is, "It is not for me to extend forgiveness. That is the responsibility of those who endured the suffering."

Harboring Malicious Thoughts

The sixth symptom is "malice", which means to harbor thoughts of revenge. This can take the form of secretly enjoying and eagerly listening to an ill report concerning the one who has caused our offence; or on hearing some bad news about the same person, wishing it could have been worse. I heard a story concerning Winston Churchill when he was Prime Minister, that one of his aides rushed up to him at the House of Commons saying, "Prime Minister, Mr Attlee has been taken ill." Mr Attlee was the leader of the Opposition at the time. On hearing the news Mr Churchill, with a twinkle in his eye, retorted, "Nothing trivial I trust."

Another expression of malice can be allowing our thoughts to imagine ways of getting our own back. This is a dangerous occupation because it can be the first step that leads a murderer to take the life of another. Certainly, malice is one of the chief motives that police look for when investigating a murder.

Malice can take the form of withholding information that could clear our adversary's good name and reputation when his character is being maligned by others. Worse than that, it can mean that we take an active part in either spreading untruths about him or passing on damaging information without first checking up to find whether that information is accurate or not. Someone has said, "An offence is like buttermilk: the longer it stands, the more sour it becomes."

Whenever someone is heard making spiteful remarks concerning another, it is almost certain that he or she is scandalized and is holding malice in their heart toward that person. As I have mentioned previously, we read in Matthew 12:34–35:

> *"... For the mouth speaks out of that which fills the heart. The good man brings out of his good treasure what is good; and the evil man brings out of his evil treasure what is evil."*

Sore Points

Symptom number seven is an unusual reaction at the mention of a name or a place associated with the offence.

Some years ago when I was pastoring a church, I found myself deeply offended with Frank, one of our senior leaders, who had requested the elders' permission and blessing to form a new house group with a view to it becoming a fresh church plant. Not only did we give it our blessing, but I warmly shared the vision with the rest of the church and invited any who felt that God was leading them in this venture to consider relocating in order to form the new group. Quite a number were excited by the vision and sold their homes in order to move into the area where the church was to be planted. Everything seemed to be progressing well until nine months later, when I received a phone call from Frank saying that God was calling him to another city, which happened to be over a thousand miles away. My first thought was about all those who had moved house and whose dreams now laid shattered. As I suspected they were all feeling down and disillusioned by the turn of events. This all happened just as a summer holiday was about to commence for Janette and me so, instead of getting our emotional tanks replenished and our spiritual batteries recharged, we started back into the autumn months' responsibilities feeling worn out and cheated of our holidays. I was not feeling a very blessed man. However, I managed to put all of this behind me and thought that my spirit was clear with Frank. A couple of years later, I was sitting in a restaurant with four other leaders and began to scan the menu when my eyes alighted on a chicken dish that carried the name of the city to which Frank had moved. Suddenly all my former feelings of annoyance and resentment towards Frank rose up inside me. I could not believe it. Clearly the matter still lay unresolved in my subconscious.

Birds of a Feather

The eighth symptom is that a person scandalized, in some mysterious way, teams up with other offended people. They begin to fellowship around their wounded souls, which in turn seems to draw them together in a kindred spirit. The causes and circumstances of the offences may be entirely different, but they include the same elements of self-pity and resentment. Someone has said, "birds of a feather flock together." People who suffer from ill-health have a strange habit of drawing comfort from others who are also troubled with frequent ailments. It is almost as if they are actually enjoying ill-health. So it is with scandalized people – they love to repeat the same old story over and over. The problem with people behaving in this manner is that, all too easily, they can become a powerful coalition of hurt people who can negatively influence a local congregation, even to the point of creating a church split. I have more than once observed the trail of havoc that an offended person has left behind as they have moved from church to church. The damage they inflict is greatly compounded if the pastor should make the mistake of acting expediently by prematurely inviting them into leadership. I remember one of the churches with which I'm linked receiving a gifted couple into the heart of the fellowship and quickly offering the husband the vacant position of church administrator. It turned out to be a serious mistake. As time went by, it was noticed that certain people who carried a grudge against the elders seemed to gravitate towards him and, after a while, ended up leaving the church. When he was challenged about some of the statements he was alleged to have made he took offence and left. Even to this day we still hear of things he is supposed to be saying against us. However, a few months ago one of our leader's wives happened to be talking to one of his relatives who said, "His troubles didn't start with you people. He never got over the trouble he had in his previous church."

Uncontrolled Anger

The ninth symptom is outbursts of anger. Volcanic eruptions occur because, underneath the earth's surface, pressure builds up that must eventually find release. If there were no pressure, there would be no eruption. I was in Vancouver, Canada, on the Sunday that Mount St Helens erupted. Although we were over 200 miles away, we could still hear the explosion and feel the earth tremor.

Three things have always fascinated me about people who frequently lose their temper: firstly, the incident that triggers the outburst is usually quite trivial and is totally disproportionate to the measure of anger expressed. Secondly, the anger seems to overspill from a reservoir extremely close to the surface and has been lying there waiting for the right moment to be expressed. The tell-tale signs of its existence were expressed in impatience, agitation and frustration. Thirdly, the person on whom the anger is unleashed is completely taken by surprise and can be anybody who just happens to be about at the time and says or does something that detonates the explosion. More often than not, it is someone close to the temper-loser such as a spouse, parent or child. However, sometimes it can be a hapless cat or dog that just happens to be in the vicinity at the wrong time, or it can be a door that's slammed, a plate that's smashed, a tin can that's kicked or a wall that is punched. Hospital casualty personnel can tell many interesting and unusual stories about people admitted for treatment to injuries sustained during such temper tantrums.

People manifesting this symptom seldom admit they are wrong, even though they may show signs of remorse and say that they are sorry. Also, because these outbursts occur so regularly, the person doing it fails to realize the seriousness of their unacceptable behavior or the relational and emotional damage they are inflicting on their loved ones, especially their children. Proverbs 25:28, says:

> *"Like a city that is broken into and without walls*
> *Is a man who has no control over his spirit."*

It is generally accepted by psychologists that uncontrolled anger such as this, is closely connected to unresolved hurts from the past. One last thing: the person displaying such behavior fails to understand that their conduct is viewed very seriously in the eyes of God. He highly commends self-control in Proverbs 16:32 when He says,

> *"He who is slow to anger is better than the mighty*
> *And he who rules his spirit, than he who captures a city."*

whereas in Galatians 5:20 he includes *"outbursts of anger"* among the deeds of the flesh.

Withdrawal Symptoms

Finally, we come to the last symptom in my list and this is the symptom of withdrawal or escapism.

Mary was engaged to be married, but four weeks before the wedding Tom her fiancé telephoned to say, "The wedding's off." Mary was devastated. "He didn't even have the decency or courtesy to tell me face to face. I will never trust another man again," she continued, "I'll never give my heart away to anyone." And she kept to her word. She was pleasant enough, but she always made sure she kept that little bit of distance between everyone else and herself.

I have met missionaries who have acknowledged that the main reason they ended up on the mission field is because they wanted to escape from the painful memories incurred through a broken relationship.

I have met people who won't get involved with a local church because of painful experiences suffered in a previous church.

Do you recognize yourself in any of the above mentioned symptoms? If you do, your response to the following chapter will more than likely determine whether you continue to remain trapped in your self-made prison, or by making the right choices, walk out into the freedom that God's heart longs for you to experience.

Chapter 9

Ten Steps to Freedom

Nobody simply drifts into a state of being scandalized. We get there by making choices, even though we may not recognize we are exercising a choice at the time. This highlights the danger of making impulsive, emotional responses when hurt. In the heat of the moment we often make decisions or say things that commit us to entrenched positions which can be almost impossible to get out of. The problem is that we feel almost compelled to say or do something. After yielding to the temptation we often experience remorse but it is now too late – the die is cast.

If it were choices that got us into the trouble, it will also be choices that get us out. With that in mind I would like to offer the following suggestions.

Step 1

The first step to freedom is to make a clear decision to bring the whole situation before Jesus and place it under His Lordship. By so doing, we humble ourselves, which in turn puts us under the promised blessing of God's grace. In 1 Peter 5:5–7 we read,

> "... GOD IS OPPOSED TO THE PROUD, BUT GIVES GRACE TO THE HUMBLE. *Therefore humble yourselves under the mighty hand of God, that He may exalt you at the proper time, casting all your anxiety upon Him, because He cares for you.*"

Step 2

The second step is to treat the situation as being extremely serious by resolving that you will do whatever is necessary to extricate yourself from the shackles that bind you to the offence. Jesus said in Matthew 18:8, 9:

> *"If your hand or your foot causes you to stumble* [which is the same as being scandalized], *cut it off and throw it from you . . . If your eye causes you to stumble, pluck it out and throw it from you."*

Remember the verse we referred to earlier from Proverbs 18:19?

> *"A brother offended is harder to be won than taking a strong city."*

Settle the issue now, that no matter how long it takes, you will pursue with dogged persistence the cleansing of your soul from this offence. Also, recognize that to continue to carry an offence is an act of disobedience, the fruit of which is self-destruction and inner torment. The Psalmist described it like this in Psalm 73:21–22:

> *"When my heart was embittered*
> *And I was pierced within,*
> *Then I was senseless and ignorant;*
> *I was like a beast before You."*

Step 3

The third step is to accept the sovereignty of God. Psalm 115:3 says,

> *"But our God is in the heavens;*
> *He does whatever He pleases."*

Sometimes, when I am feeling somewhat overwhelmed with the weight of responsibilities resting on my shoulders, I will go outside and look up into the night sky and gaze into outer space and contemplate the scientists' reports that claim they have counted over one hundred billion, billion stars, as well as one hundred billion galaxies, and that they estimate that our local galaxy contains one trillion moons. Such awesome reality has a marvelous way of drawing my little concerns into proper perspective. It helps me realize that ultimately, God is in control, Jesus has all authority in heaven and on earth, and He is the one who has the keys of death and of Hades and nothing ever happens to the child of God by mistake. Thomas Brooks in his treatise entitled *Under the Smarting Rod* (Banner of Truth) writes:

> "Men that see not God in an affliction are easily cast into a feverish fit, they will quickly be in a flame, and when their passions are up, and their hearts on fire, they will begin to be saucy, and make no bones of telling God to his teeth that they do well to be angry, Jonah 4:8–9. Such as will not acknowledge God to be the author of all their afflictions will be ready enough to fall in with that mad principle of the Manichees, who maintained the devil to be the author of all calamities; as if there could be any evil of affliction in the city and the Lord have no hand in it, Amos 3:6. Such as can see the ordering hand of God in all their afflictions, will with David, lay their hands upon their mouths, when the rod of God is laid upon their backs, 2 Samuel 16:11–12. If God's hand be not seen in the affliction, the heart will do nothing but fret and rage under affliction."

If God had not pulled back the curtains of heaven and allowed us to see the other half of the story regarding Job's trials and sufferings, we would have been left to the conclusion that it was the wicked Sabeans who had stolen the oxen and donkeys as well as murdering Job's servants with the sword; that it was a fireball falling from the sky which consumed all of Job's sheep together with their shepherds, and that it was the evil Chaldeans who stole all of his camels and killed the remaining servants. Then, when we read the account of how a tornado had struck the house in which all his sons and daughters were having a party, causing the house to collapse on top of them, killing everyone, we would probably have remarked, "How unlucky can you get?" The boils we would have put down to some virus that was going around at the time and assumed that Job's generally poor emotional state made him highly susceptible to the infection. But of course we know from Scripture that it all began with God initiating a conversation with Satan by asking him the question, *"Have you considered my servant Job?"* It was also God who twice gave permission for Satan to attack Job.

Apart from the prophet Elihu, Job's companions all misinterpreted the calamities. Elihu, on several occasions during his discourse, draws Job's attention to the vastness of God's creation – the omnipotence of His power and the omniscience of His knowledge and wisdom. In chapter 37:5–13 he says,

> *"God thunders with His voice wondrously,*
> *Doing great things which we cannot comprehend.*
> *For to the snow He says: 'Fall on the earth,'*
> *And to the downpour and the rain, 'Be strong.'*
> *He seals the hand of every man,*
> *That all men may know his work.*
> *Then the beast goes into his lair*
> *And remains in its den.*
> *Out of the south comes the storm,*
> *And out of the north the cold.*
> *From the breath of God ice is made,*
> *And the expanse of the waters is frozen.*
> *Also with moisture He loads the thick cloud;*
> *He disperses the cloud of His lightning.*
> *It changes direction, turning around by His guidance,*
> *That it may do whatever He commands it*
> *On the face of the inhabited earth.*
> *Whether for correction, or for His world,*
> *Or for lovingkindness, He causes it to happen."*

We need to settle the issue that, because of God's sovereignty, *"God causes all things to work together for good to those who love God, to those who are called according to his purpose"* (Romans 8:28).

Luther said Christ's cross "is no letter in the book, and yet it hath taught me more than all the letters in the book." Every outward negative experience has a blessing hidden within. Thomas Brooks put it this way:

> "As there is a curse wrapped up in the best things he gives the wicked, so there is a blessing wrapped up in the worst things he brings upon his own; as there is a curse wrapped up in a wicked man's health, so there is a blessing wrapped up in a godly man's sickness; as there is a curse wrapped up in a wicked man's strength, so there is a blessing wrapped up in a godly man's weakness; as there is a curse wrapped up in a

wicked man's wealth, so there is a blessing wrapped up in a godly man's wants; as there is a curse wrapped up in a wicked man's honor, so there is a blessing wrapped up in a godly man's reproach; as there is a curse wrapped up in all a wicked man's mercies, so there is a blessing wrapped up in all a godly man's crosses, losses and changes."

Once we are able to accept by faith that God is sovereign and therefore in control, then a dramatic change takes place in how we view and respond to life's painful episodes. I'm sure this is why Joseph was able to say to his brothers in Genesis 50:20:

"As for you, you meant evil against me, but God meant it for good in order to bring about this present result, to preserve many people alive."

Among those whose life was preserved was Judah, from whose tribe, as regards the humanity of Jesus, the promised Messiah was to come forth. Joseph suffered nineteen long years of rejection, false accusation and wrongful imprisonment in order to preserve the life of Judah. Joseph was able, with limited understanding, to see a small part of the reason for his sufferings but, the fact was, God had Golgotha in mind and the whole world in His heart when He allowed Joseph to pass through what must have been many dark nights of the soul.

Paul was in prison as a direct result of being persecuted by the Jews. Of course the Roman government were the ones holding him in jail, yet neither were the reason he gives for his incarceration. In Ephesians 3:1: he says, *"For this reason I, Paul, the prisoner of Christ Jesus."* He was not the prisoner of the Jews nor of the Roman Empire, but the prisoner of Jesus Christ. When we can see the hand of Jesus, it changes everything.

When I was a child and attending the local brethren assembly, I often heard the brother officiating at the "Lord's table" make this remark before breaking the bread: "Let us now enter into the sufferings of Christ." I used to wonder to myself, "What on earth does he mean?" and to be perfectly honest, I still have difficulty grasping to what the dear brother was referring. It seems to me the only way we can enter into the sufferings of Christ is by actually experiencing suffering ourselves.

Here is a testing question to consider: if I was participating in the sufferings of Christ, would I actually be aware of it? Or would I blame the devil or some unkind human?

A close friend of mine has been going through two years of what he describes as a "living hell". Three people had caused him great offence and without question he had been dealt with unjustly. Recently, he was in a meeting during which someone gave him a personal prophecy, the gist of which stated that he had been badly bruised, but his perception that he was being disciplined by God was inaccurate; the truth was that he had been participating in the sufferings of Christ. My friend immediately dissolved into tears of relief and comfort. He left that meeting a new man, free to forgive and able to release those who had wronged him.

Step 4

The fourth step is to resist self-pity. Someone has said, "We cannot afford the luxury of self-pity." How true! We need to be hard on ourselves when we find ourselves asking questions such as, "But why me?" and "What have I done to deserve this?" Sympathizing friends are no friends at all. When we are in the process of being scandalized we need friends who will find a way of reaching down inside us and who will call us up in God. Some years ago I fell quite seriously ill in Zimbabwe and found it necessary to go to a medical centre for tests. Whilst the doctor was examining me he found a lump alongside my liver. Just as I was leaving he said, "By the way, Mr Coombs, I suggest you see your family doctor immediately you arrive back in England so that he can give you a thorough examination." There was a serious note to his voice which made me feel a little nervous. "Why would that be necessary?" I asked. "Because," he said, "I found a lump on your liver and that could turn out to be a serious matter!" I knew immediately what he was hinting at. "I don't think I'm going to sleep too well tonight with that little bit of information swilling around in my mind," I commented, trying to sound casual. I will never forget his response. He looked me straight in the eye and asked, "Are you a man of faith or not?" He was brilliant. It was just the shot in the arm I needed. "You're right," I responded, "You're absolutely right."

Anxiety and self-pity provide the ideal atmosphere for Satan to work. Sometimes our well-meaning friends unwittingly serve the devil's purposes, as was the case with Peter after Jesus informed the disciples that he was going up to Jerusalem to suffer and be crucified. Matthew 16:22–23 says,

> *"Peter took Him aside and began to rebuke Him, saying, 'God forbid it, Lord! This shall never happen to You.' But He [Jesus] turned and said to Peter, 'Get behind Me, Satan! You are a stumbling block to Me; for you are not setting your mind on God's interests, but man's.'"*

Step 5

The fifth step is to receive firm counsel. Don't go seeking counsel from those who you know will be empathetic because they themselves may already scandalized. Remember, our first step was to cast our care on to Jesus our Wonderful Counselor. If further help is required, seek it from some reliable person who you know is not pragmatic or economic with the truth but principled and biblical in their counsel.

Step 6

The sixth step is to love God's law. Psalm 119:165: says,

> *"Those who love Your law have great peace,*
> *And nothing causes them to stumble."*

Jesus said in Matthew 7:24–25,

> *"Therefore every one who hears these words of Mine and acts upon them, may be compared to a wise man who built his house on the rock. And the rain fell, and the floods came, and the winds blew, and slammed against that house; and yet it did not fall, for it had been founded on the rock."*

Those floods and winds could well be interpreted as abuse, rejection, disloyalty, financial failure, slander and divorce; all are causes of offence, yet Jesus promises that all who do what He says will remain secure in the midst of life's storms. In Deuteronomy 8:3 we read, *"man lives by everything that proceeds out of the mouth of the LORD."*

God's word is not only preventative medicine but it also has miraculous restorative qualities as David points out in Psalm 19:7 where he says, *"The law of the* LORD *is perfect, restoring the soul."*

Step 7

The seventh step is to avoid thinking presumptuously. In Psalm 19:13 David asks God to keep him from *"presumptuous sins"*, in fact he goes on to say, *"Let them not rule over me."* James exhorts his readers in chapter 4:13–15:

> *"Come now, you who say, 'Today or tomorrow, we will go to such and such a city, and spend a year there and engage in business and make a profit.' Yet you do not know what your life will be like tomorrow. You are just a vapor that appears for a little while and then vanishes away. Instead you ought to say, 'If the Lord wills, we will live and also do this or that.'"*

James goes on in verse 16 to describe presumptuous behavior as "boasting in arrogance". Presumption is very similar to false expectations. You will remember that false expectations was one of the root causes for being scandalized.

Step 8

The eighth step is to keep a balanced overview. We should never measure God by one single incident. In Psalm 13 we see David struggling with his current circumstances. He asks,

> *". . . Will You forget me forever?*
> *How long will You hide Your face from me?*
> *How long shall I take counsel in my soul,*
> *Having sorrow in my heart all the day?"*   (Psalm 13:1–2)

He's not a very happy man at this stage in his life. We can also detect a little self-pity creeping in. However, he makes a choice that will save his soul from being scandalized:

> *"But I have trusted in Your lovingkindness;*
> *My heart shall rejoice in Your salvation.*
> *I will sing to the* LORD,
> *Because He has dealt bountifully with me."*   (Psalm 13:5–6)

There are always two sides to a cloud. Although Joseph was in prison for thirteen-and-a-half years, he reigned as prime minister of Egypt for eighty years. Although David was banished for at least five years, he reigned over all Israel for forty years. In Job 42:10, 12–13 we read:

> *"And the LORD restored the fortunes of Job when he prayed for his friends, and the LORD increased all that Job had twofold ... The LORD blessed the latter days of Job more than his beginning; and he had 14,000 sheep and 6,000 camels and 1,000 yoke of oxen and 1,000 female donkeys. He had seven sons and three daughters."*

Step 9

The ninth step is to choose to forgive the person or persons who have caused us so much hurt. The word "forgiveness" means to let go and to send away. It is an act of the will. It does not require great feeling and emotion although, where there have been deep wounds, especially from childhood, the relief of giving up and letting the whole thing go often results in a huge release of emotion.

Forgiveness is very big with God. Jesus has warned us of the consequences if we do not forgive those who sin against us. First of all, in Matthew 6:15, He says,

> *"But if you do not forgive others, then your Father will not forgive your transgressions."*

Secondly, in Matthew chapter 18, Jesus tells the story of the unmerciful slave, who, although he had been forgiven the impossible debt of $10,000,000, refused to forgive his fellow slave who only owed him a paltry sum of 25 cents. The slave's master, on discovering the slave's unforgiving response, is moved with anger and hands him over to the torturers (who are probably demons) until he should repay all that was owed him. Then, in verse 35, Jesus gives this solemn warning:

> *"My heavenly Father will also do the same to you, if each of you does not forgive his brother from your heart."*

Someone has said, "Forgiveness is the key that unlocks the door of resentment and the handcuffs of hate. It is a power that breaks the chains of bitterness and the shackles of selfishness."

Step 10

The tenth step is to verbalize the forgiveness. It is not enough to just make an internal decision to forgive; the forgiveness needs to be spoken. If we don't speak it out, it then becomes so easy to take it all back. I speak from personal experience. Of course, even when we do speak out our forgiveness, it does not mean we won't be tempted to resurrect the whole matter once again. However, it is much easier to stand by a decision already made and confessed than it is to bring one's self to make a decision in the first place. The longer you leave it the harder it becomes. That is one of the reasons the Bible tells us not to let the sun go down on our wrath. Many times over the past years of being a pastor, grown up children have expressed their great regret at not getting reconciled with their parents before their death. Even husbands and wives whose partner had died suddenly have, on occasions, told me that the biggest mistake they made was not to have kept current accounts in clearing past offences.

During the time I was the pastor of Basingstoke Baptist Church I received a phone call from a sixty-year-old lady asking if I would conduct her husband's funeral. Although they didn't come to our fellowship, they were Baptists and she wanted a "Baptist" service. When I visited her home to comfort her and discuss the funeral service she told me a most touching story about what happened the day her loved one passed away. That particular morning they got caught up in a most horrendous row before he left to go to work. As is usually the case, it had been a "storm in a teacup" that had got completely out of control. She said to me, "Pastor, we said things to each other that were so hateful. I can't believe we could talk to each other like that, but we did. It was a nightmare. I was in the kitchen when he eventually left for work. There were no goodbye kisses. I watched him through the kitchen window as he walked down our garden path, his head was down and his shoulders stooped over. There was no looking back as he opened the gate and began to walk along the pavement; he looked so heavy-hearted. I could stand it no longer and rushed to the back door and called out, 'Honey, come back.' He immediately turned round and came back and I could see his eyes were full of tears. We met at the gate and fell into each other's arms whispering our apologies and forgiveness and off to work he went. That night, I was standing at the kitchen sink when he came into view walking towards our back gate. I was wiping my hands before going to the door to greet him when just as he reached the gate he suddenly clutched his chest and fell to the ground. I rushed to his side but it was too late – he was gone. Pastor, he died at the very spot where we had made up our quarrel in the morning." At this point she began to sob uncontrollably. "Pastor," she eventually said, "I don't know what I would have done if we hadn't kissed and made up."

Jesus made it very clear that not only were we to forgive, but we were to do it from the heart. The Bible often links the heart and the mouth together. For example, Romans 10:10:

"for with the heart a person believes, resulting in righteousness, and with the mouth he confesses, resulting in salvation."

In closing, there are three things that I have found helpful. First, I take the decision that I am going to forgive. This amounts to an act of obedience. I may not want to do it; I may not feel like doing it, but I know I have got to do it. Second, I ask the Lord Jesus to make it a reality in my heart. Only Jesus can change my heart and bring me to the place where I actually want to do it. Third, once it has become a reality, I then wait for the Holy Spirit to show me the right moment to express my forgiveness.

Once I take the decision to offer forgiveness, I have taken the first step of the journey out of my trap. I dare you to take that risk!

Chapter 10

Coping with Bereavement

"For within the hollow crown
That rounds the mortal temples of a King
Keeps Death his court; and there the antic sits,
Scoffing his state, and grinning at his pomp;
Allowing him a breath, a little scene,
To monarchize, be fear'd, and kill with looks;
Infusing him with self and vain conceit,
As if this flesh, which walks about our life,
Were brass impregnable; and humour'd thus,
Comes at the last, and with a little pin
Bores through his castle-wall, and – farewell King!"
(William Shakespeare: *Richard II*)

When it comes to the subject of death one thing is certain: sooner or later everyone who lives out their normal life span will find themselves having to cope with the trauma of losing someone who is precious to them. Death is inevitable.

The word "bereavement" comes from the old English word *bereafian* which means "to be robbed", "to be dispossessed" and "to be left desolate".

Death is so final. There is no second chance. It is no respecter of persons, whether monarch or beggar. Death has no favorites; rich and poor, young and old, all alike, are cruelly cut off by its irresistible force. In one dreadful moment cherished plans are dashed to pieces with a sigh or a cry. The doctor says, "I'm afraid it's all over," and indeed it is, but the pain, heartache and lonely nights are only just beginning. The very thought of its permanence strikes despair into what was previously a heart full of hopes and dreams. The loss of a loved one is irretrievable; nothing is more devastating than death. Sometimes I look at my wife of forty-five years and say to myself, "I hardly know you and yet I don't know how I would be able to live without you."

Death has stabbed me in the back, leaving me with a permanent scar, on at least six occasions. The first time was thirty-nine years ago and involved the death from a brain tumor of my little three-year-old nephew Geoffrey.

At the time, Janette and I lived in a three-bedroom terraced house in Acton, a London suburb. One afternoon, my quiet nap was interrupted by the door bell ringing. On opening the door I was met by my brother Cyril and his wife Margaret. It was easy to see by the look in their eyes that something was wrong; indeed, something was terribly wrong. Once inside the door it didn't take long before their grief began to pour out. They had just come from Great Ormond Street Hospital which specializes in the treatment and care of sick children. "It's our Geoffrey. He has a brain tumor and the specialist has just told us today that there is nothing they can do." Words are never adequate to describe the frightened, desolate look in the eyes of parents whose hopes and dreams have just been shattered by the news that the precious child that they have raised thus far, is about to be cruelly snatched away from them; that some evil, destructive monster has taken up residence inside the same body that they have tenderly nurtured, nourished and cherished.

Cyril and Margaret continued to stay with us whilst they daily visited Geoffrey in hospital. A few days later they returned with a new light in their eyes and sounded quite buoyed up. "We've got some good news," they said, "the doctor is going to operate." Alas, their optimism did not last too long. The operation went reasonably well but the surgeon was unable to remove all of the malignant growth. As Cyril and Margaret both held senior positions in the nursing profession they understood perfectly well that it was only a matter of time before little Geoffrey succumbed to the cancer. Sadly, the benefit of the surgery only lasted a little over six months.

It is hard to imagine what it must be like for those who have no personal faith in Jesus. To have to cope with such a tragic loss without the Lord's strength and support must be unbearable. Cyril and Margaret, on the other hand, found that the comfort and sense of God's loving care completely lifted them above the ordeal. What happened the day on which Geoffrey died can only be described as supernatural. It was Cyril and Margaret's turn to host the monthly half-night of prayer for revival for that part of the county of Kent. The prayer meeting finally finished at about 2 am and concluded with the group that had gathered, standing up and singing the doxology, "Praise God from whom all blessings flow." In the next room the body of baby Geoffrey lay cold and lifeless.

The little chapel was packed to overflowing for the funeral service. Len Adams, who had been a missionary in the Afghan Border Crusade, gave the main address. He gave as his text Psalm 77:6: *"I will remember my song in the night."* It was powerful! He and his wife Audrey had themselves lost a child whilst they had been out in Afghanistan and Len shared the story of how his child had actually died in his arms. He told of how, when he had laid the lifeless body down beside him on the rock, that the Lord had come and wonderfully comforted him with what he called, "My song in the night." Len's words were not cheap; nor were there any platitudes; he simply extended an invitation for us to reach out to the Lord and in so doing we would discover that, even in our darkest hour, in some strange way God would put a new song in our hearts.

There is one scene that will be etched forever upon my memory: it was Margaret standing outside the chapel all alone, waiting by the hearse and watching the tiny coffin being placed inside. As the car drew slowly away she took a few steps out into the road and wistfully waved goodbye. A mother's pain! A mother's broken heart! It was too much. I quietly turned away and embraced my own silent grief. Tears spilled out that had as much to do with watching Cyril and Margaret suffer as for the loss of my nephew.

I made three unusual discoveries that wet, windy afternoon. The first was guilt! Suddenly, as I turned round to watch the hearse disappear over the brow of the hill, I felt guilty. I began to think of my own son Mark, who had been born two weeks earlier than Geoffrey. It was a powerful feeling. I found myself asking the questions, "Why is it Geoffrey is being buried today and not Mark?" "What right have I to keep my son when they have lost theirs?"

The second discovery was that whilst there was unusual grace and composure surrounding Cyril and Margaret, there was none for me! I found myself totally overwhelmed by sorrow. I actually felt a physical pain in my chest and in the middle of my back. It was so intense I felt like I was choking.

The third thing struck me whilst I was driving back to Acton. I was experiencing considerable difficulty at the time in trying to see through the windscreen because of the heavy rain pelting on to the window. Also, the problem wasn't helped by the headlights of the oncoming traffic shining directly into my eyes. Whilst all this was happening, I discovered a growing anger rising up inside me toward the other motorists traveling in the opposite direction. "They don't care," I thought to myself, "they are just going by with no thought about how I'm feeling." Illogical? Yes! Unreasonable? Certainly! But that is how I felt and that is how many others feel when they go through the same experience of grief. One widow describing her feelings as she walked around the grocery store put it this way: "Everyone was totally occupied with what they were doing. Here was I, my heart breaking! And nobody cared."

I took the next three days off work. I just couldn't bring myself to face meeting other people.

Janette and I had recently purchased a new recording featuring a Swedish singer called Einar Ekberg. One of the songs was from Ecclesiastes 3:1–8 and included the lines:

> "There is an appointed time for everything.
> And there is a time for every event under heaven.
> There's a time to give birth, and a time to die.
> . . . a time to weep and a time to laugh;
> . . . a time to mourn and a time to dance."

I couldn't get the haunting tune or words out of my head. Each time I thought of them I found myself weeping. For the first time in my life I understood a little of what others were going through when they lost a loved one. I could now empathize with them.

Four Stages of Bereavement

It is important always to bear in mind that grief is a process and not a permanent state. This knowledge in itself can be an enormous encouragement to someone who is in the early days of bereavement.

Recently I attended a seminar on the subject of bereavement

led by Eileen Wallis and Pauline Turner. During her presenta-
tion Pauline Turner pointed out that there are four stages of
bereavement.

Stage 1 – denial and disbelief

One of my duties as a police officer was to deliver what we called
"a death notice". It was one task no one wanted to do. Often
the message received at the police station failed to include the
relationship between the deceased and the person to whom you
were delivering the message, so you had no idea what to expect
when you broke the news. Some people choked on receiving the
news; others vomited; some even danced and jumped up and
down; some broke into hysterical laughter; but many times the
only response was a stunned silence. The first funeral at which I
was asked to officiate involved a man who had died tragically
from injuries received through falling off a ladder at work. The
dead man's eldest son took charge of all the funeral arrange-
ments and seemed to be completely composed and emotionally
stable – that was, until the time arrived for the final act of
interment. We had all gathered around the grave and the
undertakers commenced to let down the coffin into the ground.
Suddenly, to everybody's utter astonishment he tried to jump
into the grave and had to be forcibly restrained by the other
members of his family. Looking back at the situation it is
obviously clear that, up until the moment of interment, he had
been in a state of denial. The sight of his father's coffin being
lowered out of sight finally convinced him that this was for real.

Eileen Wallis shared at the same seminar of how she reacted to
the news of her husband Arthur's sudden death. She described
her feelings as "total shock", "numbed" and "emotions frozen".
She said, "It was so unreal." These are common responses in
people who are trying to come to terms with the sudden news of
their loved one's death. However, we need to be careful not to
jump to the conclusion that denial is something that necessarily
goes away within a few weeks of the loved one's death. In
Bereavement published by Pelican books, the author, Colin
Murray Parkes, points out that, during the case studies of
twenty-two London widows, even a year after bereavement over
half of them still said that there were times when they could not
believe what had happened. "It's like a dream. I feel I'm going to
wake and it'll be alright. He'll be back again."

Stage 2 – anger and sadness

This anger can be expressed in various forms and directed towards any number of different people, including the deceased. One widow got absolutely furious with her husband for being so inconsiderate as to die just a few weeks before their first child was born, thus leaving her to raise the baby all alone. Doctors, nurses, employers and especially relatives can all find themselves in the firing line. People who are on the receiving end of such outbursts of anger should be mature and sensible enough to realize that such expressions are only momentary and carry very little substance to them.

Sometimes this state of anger and sadness can be entered into within twenty-four hours. Such was the case for me with the death of three-year-old Sharon. Within a few hours of her death, I drove her parents, Howard and Carole, from Basingstoke to Maidstone in Kent to stay with a loving Christian family who I knew would surround them with compassion and care. Howard and Carole were like a son and daughter to Janette and me. I felt their pain more deeply than anything I could remember. It broke my heart just to stand by and watch their hearts being broken. The following day (which was a Sunday) I found myself experiencing overwhelming anger as I returned to Basingstoke. I remember banging my fist on the steering wheel of the car and shouting at God, "But why God? Why? Why?" I felt so distraught. My speed began to increase and my judgment decreased as I overtook cars in places where the Highway Code warns a motorist not to, such as junctions, the brow of hills and approaching bends. Whilst commencing to overtake another car on one such bend, I suddenly found myself careering toward a van speeding at me from the opposite direction. I slammed on the brakes and steered the car back into my own lane, but in so doing I lost complete control of the steering. My car ended up doing a full turn in the middle of the road. Feeling somewhat foolish and scared, I pulled myself together and slowly completed the journey back home. In the evening I visited Slough Gospel Tabernacle where the late Billy Richards was the pastor. In the middle of the service Billy introduced a song, the singing of which opened my emotional floodgates and released me to freely cry without worrying about what anyone thought – something I had been unable to do up to that point. The song was:

"His name is Jesus, Jesus,
Sad hearts weep no more.
He heals the broken hearted,
Opens wide the prison door.
He is able to deliver, evermore."

We must have sung the song at least fifteen times and at the
end of the service we returned to the same song and continued to
sing it for another ten minutes. It was just what was needed. I
uncontrollably bawled my eyes out. However, even on the way
home that night, the anger was beginning to rise again. My speed
increased and for the second time that day I only just managed to
avoid a head-on collision whilst overtaking on a bend.

On Thursday we buried little Sharon's body. There is one piece
of counsel I will always regret giving. I advised Howard and Carol
that in order to protect themselves from further trauma, it might
be best if they stayed in Maidstone rather than return to attend
the funeral. They had already suffered the death of seventeen-
day-old baby Matthew, only two months previously and I
erroneously thought that their presence at little Sharon's funeral
would be too much for them to bear. Unfortunately they took
my advice and as a result were robbed of a very important part of
the grieving process.

Jean Richardson writing about the significance of the funeral
in her excellent book *A Death in the Family* published by Lion
Publishing, says,

> "Every bereaved person dreads this ordeal, but, whatever
> form this final ceremony takes, from a psychological point
> of view it is important. Even quite young children should be
> included in this public act of mourning. The funeral helps to
> impress the fact that death has taken place and the need to
> come to terms with what has happened. Much comfort is
> drawn from the gathering together of family, friends and
> neighbors. It brings home the reality of the situation when
> the mind is still numb enough to be protected from all the
> implications."

It was decided to hold a simple service gathered around the
graveside. When I got to the cemetery, even though I was ten
minutes early, Sharon's little white coffin was already placed

over the grave. It didn't take me long to realize that the undertakers were in a hurry to get our service over with as soon as possible in order to take their leave to process another funeral elsewhere. Once again anger rose up inside. I was livid and told the director in no uncertain terms what I thought about his inordinate haste. In some ways their insensitive, unprofessional behavior was a mixed blessing. Whilst it made me angry, at the same time it provided a diversion and an outlet for my severely strained emotions.

Stage 3 – depression

Depression usually sets in within four to six weeks after the burial, although one widow I talked to found herself going into depression four years after her husband's death. At the heart of her depression was the hopeless feeling of loneliness and the absence of the spontaneous fun they once enjoyed together. She said, "It finally dawned on me that I was going to be lonely for the rest of my life – that there was nothing to look forward to." Interestingly, it was this sense of hopelessness that caused her to turn to the Lord and come to faith in Christ. She has since remarried and borne two more children. Actually, I can hear their voices in the next room whilst I am typing this chapter.

The first two stages we have mentioned seem to have a measure of relief in them: denial helps to keep the full reality of the loss at a distance; anger has a similar effect in that it provides an outlet for pent-up emotion. However, depression is like a fog that slowly creeps up and envelopes you. Signposts vanish, perspective is lost, motivation ceases, indecision rules the day. You cannot pray or read your Bible; there is no longer anything worth looking forward to; it is like a paralysis of the mind. People who are in depression frequently become detached from everything else that is going on around them – for instance, one mother remained a recluse for nearly five years following the death of her teenage son. She found it impossible to leave the house and face all her neighbors.

This season of depression can be an extremely dangerous time, especially if the bereaved person has recently changed jobs, moved house or has been suffering from stress-related anxiety. A combination of three or more such experiences can seriously destabilize a person, even to the point of them contemplating suicide as an option. This is one of those times in a person's life where it is imperative for them to get help urgently from their pastor or doctor.

Stage 4 – acceptance

Acceptance is evidenced by the bereaved person making a conscious decision to stop looking back all the time and to start to face the future, knowing it will be without the companionship of their loved one. Some people may find that this is only possible after the first anniversary of the death. It is important that the bereaved person settle the issue that, in order for them to continue with the rest of their life, they will sooner or later have to come to this crucial turning point. Put another way, they may not yet be ready to be "willing" but they may find they are able to bring themselves to be willing to be willing.

Jean Richardson, writing from her own experience as a widow, points out the following eight characteristics/stages of grief. She explains that these will vary in their order and may overlap.

Stage 1:
Shock, which can involve muscular weakness, emptiness and inner tension.

Stage 2:
Numbness; everything seems unreal and remote.

Stage 3:
Struggle between fantasy and reality, you find reality difficult to accept and may act partly as though it had not happened.

Stage 4:
Feelings of guilt, panic or frenzy; you may want to withdraw from the outside world and even your own family.

Stage 5:
Depression, which is quite natural and to be expected.

Stage 6:
Release, shedding of tears or release of a flood of grief.

Stage 7:
Painful memories; you find yourself able to face memories and accept them.

Stage 8:
Acceptance; your new life begins and plans for the future
form. Practical and emotional problems become easier to
deal with.

Unfortunately the manner in which Western society handles
death does not offer a lot of assistance to those who are walking
through these stages.

The Sanitization of Death in the Western World

When I was a young lad, respect for the deceased and sensitivity
towards the bereaved was much more commonplace than it is
today. For instance, it was quite normal to see a notice in a shop
window saying: "This shop is closed for business today due to
the sad death of A.N. Other, one of its esteemed employees." The
rest of the staff would wear black armbands for at least seven days
after the funeral. If a neighbor passed away, the rest of the
neighborhood would lower their blinds or draw their curtains
until after the funeral. If they were not attending the funeral, the
inhabitants of each house would gather at the front of their
house. As the hearse passed by, the women would slowly lower
their heads and the men would remove their hats. Even the
undertakers would carry out their duties at a slower pace. For
instance, once all the mourners were in the cars, the funeral
director would lead the procession of vehicles on foot and
bareheaded, until they had turned the corner into the next
street. Quite often, if the chapel was close by the home of the
deceased, there would only be the hearse conveying the coffin;
everyone else would walk. Even police officers would salute the
deceased as the cortege passed by. These days death is so private
and the quicker we can get on with life the better. Life seems to
have become cheap, but to the bereaved the pain is as big today
as it has always been – it is simply that society in general has
neither the time nor the inclination to slow down enough to
properly offer condolences and care like it used to do.

Another problem that hinders proper grieving is the habit of
keeping our emotions under control. British stoicism, for
instance, should be viewed as a curse and not as a virtue. The
"stiff upper lip" is viewed by many in the medical profession as
a destructive force. When those who ought to be comforting a

grieving person withdraw, or behave as if everything should carry on as usual, they place an incredible pressure on the bereaved to pull themselves together and put on a brave face. This results in the internalization of their sorrow. Unfortunately this causes both psychological as well as physical damage.

When Jacob died (see Genesis 50:1–10), we read in verse 1 that *"Joseph fell on his father's face, and wept over him and kissed him."*

This was followed by forty days during which the physicians embalmed the body. After this the Egyptians wept for Jacob seventy days. Then, Joseph requested permission from Pharaoh to bury his father back in the land of Canaan. How long the journey took we are not told, but we do know that when they arrived at the threshing floor of Atad, *"they lamented there with a very great and sorrowful lamentation; and he observed seven days mourning for his father"* (verse 10).

The whole process of public grieving covered well in excess of four months.

The Irish at least provide an opportunity for people to gather in a formal way to share their condolences with the bereaved. I met a man recently who was traveling on the same flight as myself from Vancouver, Canada to London. He was on his way to a close relative's funeral in the Republic of Ireland and mentioned that they would be holding a "wake" for the deceased. "What happens at a 'wake'?" I enquired.

"Well," he said, "relatives and friends come to the house and sit around the coffin and reminisce about the good times they enjoyed together. Sometimes the coffin will be open. Of course, everyone will have a drink or two." He continued, "The first wake I ever attended, I couldn't believe my eyes. As I walked into the room, the first thing that caught my attention was the deceased sitting upright at the table with a deck of cards in his hand. He loved to play cards. How they managed to fix him up like that I will never know." He was convinced that the wake was a great way of providing support and encouragement to the grieving family.

Before writing this chapter I interviewed several people who had lost close relatives – amongst whom was one whose spouse committed suicide, one whose wife suddenly collapsed and died in his arms, and a couple whose eleven-year-old son died of leukemia. Their observations and advice have been extremely helpful. The seven most common mistakes people made in handling them in their bereavement were:

1. **Embarrassment.** Some folk would do anything to avoid talking to the bereaved about their loved one's death. No opportunity was given to say what led up to the loved one's death, or to recall the final moments or last words spoken. The words spoken by Malcolm to Macduff in Shakespeare's play *Macbeth* are powerfully true: "Give sorrow words, the grief that does not speak, knits up the o'erwrought heart and bids it break."

2. **Physical avoidance.** Some people, even close friends, could be noticed crossing to the other side of the road rather than meet face to face with the bereaved.

3. **Unhelpful platitudes.** "Time's a great healer ... You're young, you'll get over this ... He's with the Lord ... You wouldn't want her to suffer, would you?" Some of these platitudes may be true, but they can sound awfully cheap.

4. **Too many "helpful" books on the subject of healing prior to the loved one's death.** Add to this those who presented formulaic prayers of faith to be confessed out loud by the terminally ill. One person near to death was heard crying and saying, "I'm too weak to read these out loud. I hope God won't be mad at me."

5. **People criticizing how the bereaved expressed their sorrow,** or how they seemingly failed to show their sorrow enough. The guests at one funeral were horrified because the parents of the deceased honored their son's request for his funeral to be more like a celebration and party.

6. **People expressing their anger that God had failed to answer their prayers in not healing the one who had died.** Some even spoke of losing their faith.

7. **Feeling that within a few weeks everyone had forgotten what had happened** and that even to mention their loved one's name would be inappropriate.

The Hardest Things to Cope With

In answer to the question, "What was the hardest thing to cope with?" they gave the following answers:

1. **The loss of their loved one's future.** The couple whose eleven-year-old son had died, put it like this: "There would be no recognition of his academic or athletic achievements;

no marriage and therefore no grandchildren through him;
no more leisure or fun times together; no more enjoying his
growth or seeing his potential being realized, either spiritually or naturally."

2. **The feeling of having been robbed.** The empty space in
bed and the vacant chair at the meal table. There would no
longer be the warm embrace and the giving and receiving of
sexual pleasure. No more recounting of the day's events
around a meal. Gone was the listening ear into which they
could dump their true feelings and opinions, however nasty
or un-Christ-like they may have sounded.

3. **The feeling of guilt.** Everyone I interviewed felt regret
over one thing or another – the most common being
that they had not done enough. Even my mother who
remained faithfully by my father's side during the last
hours of his life and who, at the moment of his passing,
was holding his hand and thanking God for all the years
they had enjoyed together, mentioned to me on my last
visit with her that she wished she could have done more
for him in his last moments on earth – and she said this
nineteen years after his death. One sister felt guilty for
fighting her brother. She also felt guilty for being jealous
about the attention he received in his sickness and sub-
sequent death.

4. **The feeling of loneliness.** This was especially true for
widows and widowers. They soon discovered that much of
their social life depended on having a partner. Foursomes
are far more popular than threesomes. The seating arrange-
ments in restaurants and even church banquets are usually
in twos, fours, sixes and eights. One young widow told of
how she was re-seated three times by the hostess because
they needed her space for a couple. Couples normally like to
be seated opposite another matching couple.

This problem of suddenly finding yourself alone and un-
useful is particularly evident in the case of the widows of
leaders. One widow whose husband had been the pastor,
and who was succeeded by his son, still found she was left
out. Even the women in the church who had frequently
sought her counsel and prayers no longer approached her
for help. It was as if her ministry and usefulness died when
her husband died.

The stark reality of feeling "alone" was especially painful in a number of "firsts": the first meal alone; the first visit to a restaurant alone; the first attendance at a church service alone; the first bank statement with his or her name no longer included; the church address book no longer carrying both names; the first Christmas; the first birthday; the first wedding anniversary. Loneliness is probably the hardest part of bereavement.

5. **Getting through the night**. The Bible talks about weeping lasting for a night. People describe intense emotional anxiety as "the dark night of the soul". Undoubtedly, the experience of sorrow is at its severest during the night hours when all is silent. There is nothing to distract the griever; no chance that the phone may ring; no possibility that some-one might knock at the door. The church clock chiming every fifteen minutes only adds to the sense of time being slowly played out. The sound of the dawn chorus and the first glimpses of sunrise bring some sort of respite, but then a new problem arises: how will I be able to cope with today and all its challenges?

6. **The sense of inadequacy and insecurity**. I was present in the mortuary with one lady, who, whilst stroking her dead husband's face, kept repeating, "But what am I going to do without you? How am I going to cope? Who's going to pay the bills?" He had only passed away thirty minutes previously, but already she was realizing how much she had depended on him. This was a very real experience for me when my own father passed away, even though I was thirty-nine years old and my father was eighty-six. Although I had not sought his counsel for quite a considerable time, I still felt strangely aware that I had lost a trusted friend whose distilled wisdom was no longer available to me.

7. **The constant reminders of the loved one**. Sometimes it is the familiar smell of her perfume or his aftershave lotion; the mention in the newspaper or on the television of a place that carries a special memory; a favorite tune being played, that draws the comment, "That was our tune." One lady was walking down the street when suddenly, standing immediately in front with his back toward her, was her late husband. Just at that moment the man turned and she was able to see her mistake, but for a split second she had

been genuinely convinced that it was her man. I heard Myrtle Dobson, the mother of James Dobson, speak of the same experience on her son's radio program, *Focus on the Family*. She recited the following verse addressed to her late husband:

"I thought I saw you today, standing,
with your hands in your pockets, laughing,
the wind, playing mischievously with your hair.
My heart lunged towards you as you disappeared,
leaving a total stranger standing there.
How could I have imagined that man,
to be my darling, my precious darling?"

Before I move on to the next chapter, let me add one more thought. There are no quick remedies for the grieving soul. Nothing can bring our loved ones back to us. As Eileen Wallis said to me, "It is not true to say 'time heals'. Time doesn't heal. God heals."

I cannot put it better than Hattie M. Conrey:

"What though all my heart is yearning
    For the loved of long ago
Bitter lessons sadly learning
    From the shadowy page of woe!
If I've Jesus, 'Jesus only,'
    He'll be with me to the end;
And, unseen by mortal vision,
    Angels bands will o'er me bend."

The same thought is expressed in another hymn written by C.D. Martin:

"Lonely or sad, from friends apart,
    God will take care of you!
He will give peace to your aching heart,
    God will take care of you!"

Chapter 11

Recovering from Bereavement

We turn now to what some people describe as, "The journey back". We noticed in the last chapter that bereavement is a process. The same is true for those recovering from bereavement. It is also a matter of making the correct choices at the right time. Again, I want to point out that much of what is shared in these chapters on bereavement comes from interviewing those who have been through the valley. The following is a list of choices they made which greatly helped in their restoration.

1. Bring it all to Jesus
He sends out an invitation in Matthew 11:28:

> *"Come to Me, all who are weary and heavy-laden, and I will give you rest."*

We are told in Psalm 46:1:

> *"God is our refuge and strength,*
> *A very present help in trouble."*

Someone has translated *"a very present help"* as "abundantly available for help".

Probably the most difficult, painful funeral service I ever conducted involved a married couple, Simon and Marcia. Janette and I loved them dearly; they were like a son and daughter. Marcia entered into what can only be described as a period of deep depression. After several months, small signs of recovery seemed to be appearing and Simon began to sense that things were turning for the better. One morning, as he was leaving to take their children to school, he was particularly pleased to see Marcia follow them to the door and cheerfully send them off with a wave. What he didn't realize was, this was her last farewell. When he returned home, having only been away for a short while, he found her dead. She had taken her own life. I was in Canada on a fishing holiday at the time. On hearing the news, I caught the first flight out and returned to England. Simon, as I expected, asked me to take the funeral. Quite apart from the added difficulty of choosing the right words for the sermon, bearing in mind that Marcia had taken her own life, I also had to struggle with my own emotions over losing someone who I had grown to love dearly. Fifteen minutes before the service I met in the vestry with another pastor who, because Marcia's family were French-speaking, was going to interpret my message into French. He wanted me to go through the main points of my sermon and therefore help him with his task of interpreting. I could hardly get a sentence out without choking up in tears. Finally he had to leave in order to welcome the French-speaking guests. Now I was all alone with the overwhelming burden of conducting the service resting like a ton weight on my shoulders. "I can't do it, I can't do it," I sobbed. Then it came to me to open my Bible to see if there might be some word or verse that would help me. The page fell open at Psalm 55:22:

*"Cast your burden upon the L*ORD *and He will sustain you."*

I cannot tell you adequately what that verse meant to me. All I can say is that it perfectly answered my need. I knew the Lord was going to help me. I knew everything was going to be alright. With immense relief I cried out, "Oh, I do, I do cast my burden on to You Lord Jesus." The Lord kept His promise and did indeed sustain me. The Lord was also sustaining Simon and his young children. I will always remember the unusual grace God gave to me, that allowed me to look directly into their sad, bewildered eyes and say the Aaronic blessing from Numbers 6:24–26:

*"The L*ORD *bless you, and keep you;*
*The L*ORD *make His face shine upon you,*
And be gracious to you;
*The L*ORD *lift up His countenance on you,*
And give you peace."

Chrissy Chapman, from Cheam Community Church, is a missionary serving in Burundi. During the civil war, she visited the refugee camps daily with large amounts of porridge oats, endeavoring to feed as many children as possible. On one such visit, having emptied all the containers, she was just about to leave the camp when she happened to notice an elderly man squatting on the ground holding up a plastic mug and appearing to be praying. Chrissy turned aside to speak to him and discovered that he was eighty-five years old, and that all his known family had been slaughtered in the massacre, including his wife, his grown-up children, grandchildren and great-grandchildren. On top of this, he had not eaten for a week. Sadly, there was nothing Chrissy could give him. As she turned to leave, he called her back. "Missy missionary," he said, "I only discovered Jesus was all I needed, when Jesus was all I had."

2. Give in to grief

It is spiritually profitable for the bereaved to give expression to their sorrow. We read in Psalm 34:18, that *"The Lord is near to the broken-hearted."* And in 2 Corinthians 1:3–4: *"... the ... God of all comfort, who comforts us in all our affliction ... "*

It is good physically. People who remain stoic and refuse to let go remain tense, anxious and often depressed. It is not unusual for them to suffer severe tension-headaches or eventually to develop chronic indigestion and to lose their appetite, resulting in weight loss.

It is emotionally therapeutic. Sorrow is love being expressed in a tangible form. We always feel better after a good cry. We feel energized to face another few hours. Later on we find it becomes a few days and then a few weeks – so the slow process of recuperation quietly and at times imperceptibly, takes its steady course.

It is helpful socially. It releases others to be free to show their sorrow. It also helps your friends not to worry for your health. People get concerned if they perceive a bereaved person is "bottling it all up inside".

3. Take your time; don't hurry the process

Do not be trapped by the perception, false or otherwise, that you have got to quickly pull yourself together and look cheerful all the time.

4. At the same time restrain yourself from always talking about your loss

When you do unload, and it is vital that you do, try to make sure it is with someone who will be understanding, such as a pastor or a close friend. It is especially helpful if it is someone who has passed through the same experience. Empathy is so much superior to sympathy.

5. Make a conscious and determined decision to forgive anybody who has done or said things that you have found insensitive and hurtful

Or maybe the opposite is the case – maybe they have failed to say or do what you think ought to be expected during a time of bereavement. It could be your in-laws, the officiating minister, the doctor, even yourself. Forgiveness brings freedom and keeps your spirit sweet and gentle.

6. Make a determined effort to be outgoing

As soon as you are able, write an appreciation to as many people as possible for the cards and flowers received. If it is easier by phone and not a long-distance call then use the phone. Get into the daily habit of saying a thank-you for the smallest service rendered. The longer you leave it, the harder it becomes to re-enter the normal interaction of life. God has a plan for your life that will help make a difference wherever you go.

I told one couple, Howard and Carole, who had lost both their children in the short space of two months that they could withdraw and let Satan fill their hole with bitterness or they could let Jesus fill that hole and receive a powerful and effective ministry to others. Whenever I come across a couple who have lost a child, I send a message to Howard and Carole asking them to drop a line to the grieving parents. By so doing they are passing on the comfort that they themselves received when they traveled through their own valley experience. We read in 2 Corinthians 1:3–4,

> *"Blessed be the God and Father of our Lord Jesus Christ, the Father of mercies and God of all comfort, who comforts us in all our affliction so that we will be able to comfort those who are in any affliction with the comfort with which we ourselves are comforted by God."*

If it is at all possible, respond affirmatively to every invitation extended, whether it be meals, weddings, parties or just a cup of coffee.

7. As soon as you are able, choose a day to start disposing of your loved one's clothes and effects

Jean Richardson, who has been referred to earlier and is herself a widow, recommends that you do this as soon as possible. She also said:

> "If you can't face it alone, ask a member of the family or a close friend to help you with it. The longer you put it off, the more you will dread it and it will be at the back of your mind all the time."

Jean Richardson also warns against turning a bedroom or a chair into a shrine. It is not uncommon for parents who have lost a child to keep the youngster's bedroom exactly the way it was for many years. This can only prolong the agony.

Clothes, in good condition, are always much appreciated by those who minister to the poor, especially those who are currently involved in relief work in the third world. It also gives that extra little comforting thought that at least some good is coming out of your painful loss – someone, somewhere, is being helped.

8. Reach a firm resolve not to make hasty decisions

All the people I have heard speak on this subject have given the same advice: "Refrain from making any major decisions for at least a year. Better still, try and make it two years."

9. Make sure you are a functioning part of a spiritual family

If you belong to a church which runs house groups, endeavor to be a regular participating member. Your attendance and support will be a great encouragement to the leader. Go to each meeting with the attitude of "Lord, I make myself available to You for You to use me to be a blessing in any way You see fit." If people are in the habit of giving you a hug, be certain to give them a hug back.

10. Deal with self-pity as if it is your worst enemy

Eugenia Price writes in *Getting Through the Night* (Triangle/SPCK),

"But somehow, as long as the sun shines, even as long as we can remember that it is up there shining through an overcast day, the human heart – if it is not bound and locked by self-pity – leaps toward the light."

She continues,

"What is self-pity? Why is self-pity the only absolute block to God's activity on our behalf? The answers are so simple, I feel, as to seem ridiculous at first glance: self-pity clutches itself to itself. Self-pity cannot receive, even from God. Its hands are clenched. God waits for an open heart, an open attitude, unclenched hands. Self-pity turns inward, draws its blinds against the light – shuts out even love. Self-pity cries out, 'If I can't have the love I lost, I don't want any at all!' Self-pity screams, 'Leave me alone. I don't intend to be hurt again like this.'"

Let me say one final thing in closing this chapter. I have consulted at least a dozen books on the subject of bereavement. I have talked with a considerable number of people who have suffered the loss of loved ones. I have also drawn on thirty years of pastoral experience in counseling and comforting the sorrowing, yet, I feel as if these two chapters are so inadequate. I offer them to those of you who are presently in the middle of your dark night of the soul in the hope that you may find them some small help. You may be questioning whether God is really there and if He is, does He even care? You may even feel similar feelings to those of C.S. Lewis who said this after Joy, his wife, passed away:

"Talk to me about the truth of religion and I'll listen gladly. Talk to me about the duty of religion and I'll listen submissively. But don't come talking to me about the consolations of religion or I shall suspect that you don't understand."

Maybe C.S. Lewis was right – maybe I don't understand. But I would be woefully remiss if I failed to commend to you my extraordinary heavenly Father who is *"the God of all comfort"* and who perfectly understands our grief when we lose a loved one. A friend of mine was on one occasion angrily asked the question, "Where was God when my wife died?" My friend responded gently, "God was in the same place that He was when His own Son died at Calvary." We do have a God who cares and understands – we really, really do!

Chapter 12

The Challenge of Divorce

The way in which divorce is trivialized on television and in films would give one the impression that the ending of a marriage is no big deal. Government, particularly in Britain, have not helped matters either, for by making divorce much easier and faster to acquire, they have sent out a message that says, "Let us relieve you of the stressful responsibility and challenge of upholding the covenantal vows you made on your wedding day. Marriage isn't that important anyway." Added to this, numerous high-profile media figures – celebrities, sportspeople, politicians and even member of the Royal family – do not set a good example for the next generation of eligible newly-weds to emulate. They seem to carry on with their lives as if nothing much has really happened. However, for those of us whose unenviable task it is to seek to reassemble people's broken lives – who have the responsibility of helping people cope with the trauma of a broken marriage – the picture is entirely different.

Herbert Carson, writing in his book *Facing Suffering* (Evangelical Press), says this:

> "To put the pain of an unhappy marriage in the same bracket as the suffering of prolonged illness, or the sorrow of bereavement, may seem to some to be a serious over-statement."

But he goes on later to say,

> "Indeed I would go as far as to say that in some ways a broken marriage is a far more bitter grief than even the crushing sorrow of bereavement. This is not in any way to minimize bereavement, for it is quite a devastating experience. To lose a loved partner through death is to be left with

memories which, though they bring pain, also by their sweetness bring some solace. But to lose a partner through adultery or desertion is to face the same kind of loneliness as bereavement, but with memories whose bitterness makes the loneliness even more acute."

I am fully aware that many who read this book will want to know where I stand on the issue of divorce and remarriage. I will attempt to state my position as succinctly as possible, but the main purpose of this chapter is not to present my theology. Rather it is to try and help those who have already passed the point of no return. I will endeavor to present the biblical ideal, but also handle the biblical "real".

Early in my pastoral ministry a young couple, Brian and Tina, asked if they could come and talk to me about their common-law marriage arrangement. Brian explained that, within a week of his marriage, his wife Jean had left him and had gone to live with his best friend who had also been best man at his wedding. Some time later he met up with Tina with whom he was now living. He was still legally married to Jean, although a divorce was in process with a decree nisi having been granted, but they were still waiting for the decree absolute which was due in six weeks' time. To make matters a little more complicated, Brian and Tina now had a little three-year-old daughter. Let me backtrack a little in order for you to understand my pastoral predicament. Two years after Brian and Tina moved in together, they met someone who introduced them to Jesus Christ and they became committed Christians. They decided from that moment on that it was wrong for them to sleep together and so they ceased having a sexual relationship, although for the sake of their daughter they thought it best that they remained under the same roof. They couldn't marry because, as you will remember, Brian was still married to Jean. One other piece in the puzzle that complicated the situation still further was that Jean and her live-in boyfriend, David, had also become Christians through the witness of Brian and Tina, and now all four were close friends who met together regularly for Bible study and prayer. Furthermore, although Brian no longer had any emotional love or physical attraction for Jean, he was willing, if I so ruled, for them to renew the marriage relationship. I had once heard Billy Graham say, "You cannot unscramble scrambled egg!"

Naturally I refused to respond straight away with an answer, for the simple reason I didn't have one. But after prayer and sharing the problem with my fellow elders we arrived at the following conclusion: First of all, we believed the marriage situation had passed the point of no return – it was indeed scrambled egg. Secondly, we recognized that when a person comes to Christ and is spiritually reborn, the past is blotted out, with the exception of restitution as part of true repentance (where it applies) and where the law of the land still requires justice to be executed for crimes committed. Thirdly, we established that both couples were committed to walk out the biblical covenant of marriage if they were to be legally married in the future. Fourthly, we strongly counseled David and Jean to cease living with each other until they were married, but we felt that Brian and Tina had probably made the right decision to remain under the same roof for the sake of their daughter.

Some people, I know, will not be pleased with our conclusion that new birth blots out the consequences of past divorce. However, the argument seemed incongruous to us that someone could have sexual relations (*"become one flesh"*, 1 Corinthians 6:16) with two or three hundred different partners prior to becoming a Christian, and then immediately they came to faith in Christ were free to marry another Christian because they had not broken a "marriage covenant"; yet a Christian who had broken his marriage vows as an unbeliever and was subsequently divorced, would still carry the consequences of that past sin for his entire Christian life and be prohibited from remarriage.

My understanding of God's rules and attitudes pertaining to divorce is as follows: First and foremost, God hates the whole idea of divorce. In Malachi 2:15–16 He says, *"Do not break faith with the wife of your youth. I hate divorce"* (NIV).

Jesus said in Matthew 19:6, *"What therefore God has joined together, let no man separate."*

The Lord is a covenant-making, covenant-keeping God. Everything He does or says is within the framework of covenant. Covenant is one of the undergirding foundation stones of life, ordained by God to ensure peace, prosperity and stability for human society. Marriage is a covenant between two people. When divorce takes place, it means that covenant has been broken and human society suffers as a result. I was once escorted on a tour of a juvenile remand institution in Kent, England by the prison governor. As I was about to leave he turned to me and said, "Let me tell you an interesting piece of information: presently, there is not one boy in this place who doesn't come from a broken home." God's ideal is: marriage is for always.

George W. Peters writes in his very helpful book, *Divorce and Remarriage* (Chicago: Moody), "The God who promulgates the highest and noblest ideals cannot legislate lower and lesser ideals, though he may permit man to live and to operate on a sub-ideal level."

The Pharisees, trying to catch Jesus out, asked the question in Matthew 19:7,

> *"'Why then did Moses command to* GIVE HER A CERTIFICATE OF DIVORCE AND SEND *her* AWAY?'

Jesus replied,

> *'Because of your hardness of heart Moses permitted you to divorce your wives; but from the beginning it has not been this way.'"*
> (Matthew 19:8)

In a nutshell, if a person's spouse commits adultery, the innocent party has a legal right to divorce the guilty partner and be free to remarry. Matthew 19:9:

> *"And I say to you, whoever divorces his wife, except for immorality, and marries another woman commits adultery."*

However, God's desire would be for the victim to draw from the Lord's reservoir of forgiving grace and extend mercy and forgiveness to the erring one.

God also allows divorce and remarriage for a spouse whose partner leaves them and refuses to return because they have become a believer:

> *"Yet if the unbelieving one leaves, let him leave; the brother or the sister is not under bondage in such cases, but God has called us to peace."*
> (1 Corinthians 7:15)

I believe a wife can leave and divorce her husband for his violent behavior towards her, but I cannot see from Scripture that this then releases her to remarry. Of course, it is almost certain that he will remarry or fall into adultery, in which case she would be free to remarry.

Basically, I believe the Scriptures teach that anyone who divorces and remarries other than for immorality and desertion is committing adultery.

Let us return to the main purpose of this chapter which is to try to answer the question: How do I cope with divorce? And how can I return to normal life without being filled with resentment and bitterness?

First of all, let us establish that although it may require an Herculean effort, it can be done. The following stories are absolutely true except that the names have been changed. Within these accounts are, I believe, the keys to survival and recovery following a divorce.

I first met Patricia the evening that she made a clear commitment to Christ. She was a schoolteacher in one of the local schools and had moved to our town to get away from her husband who was also a schoolteacher and had been having an affair with one of his pupils. The first occasion he got involved with this girl was when she was only twelve years old. When Patricia discovered what was happening, she was devastated but was willing to forgive him and make a new start to their marriage. Two years later she found out that he was again sleeping with the same girl; once again she forgave him. A year later he was back to his same old ways; this time, however, his response was: "Take it or leave it. I'm going to sleep with whoever I want to. If you want to stay with me, that's fine, but I intend to have a good time."

This was the final straw for Patricia. She moved out of their home and found a new teaching post in our town.

Patricia's faith took off like a rocket. She attended every available meeting and grew into a solid, Bible-based, Spirit-filled Christian. One day she said to me, "What am I to do with my marriage?" I returned the question with a question: "What do you think you should do?" I was deeply impressed with her mature answer: "Well, the Bible says we are to forgive. So I am willing, if he is willing, to give it another chance." And that is how Frank came to visit me to talk about a reconciliation. We were having quite a pleasant chat, that is, until we came to the matter of whether he was willing to get back together with

Patricia. "Sure I am," he asserted, "but I'm not going to be tied down to her moral standards."

"That's your final word?" I asked.

"Yes, that is my final word" he replied.

Patricia, with the elder's full release and blessing, eventually filed for divorce. With God's strength, she truly forgave Frank and continued to carefully guard her heart from all resentment and bitterness. Today she is happily married to a Bible College professor and is the proud mother of four children.

Trudy had been one of the flower people of the late sixties. She and her husband Fred were pot-smokers and generally behaved in an irresponsible, free-thinking manner. She described their life-style as "bohemian". Fred was also an alcoholic. On her own admission Trudy did many things of which she was profoundly ashamed. Eventually she and Fred parted, leaving her with an eighteen-month-old child. One day, not long after they separated, she met a man at an Alcoholics Anonymous meeting who told her that he had asked Christ into his heart. He in turn introduced her to an older man who, over four days, took her through a book called *The Four Spiritual Laws*. At the end he invited her to receive Christ into her life. To her surprise, she found herself readily responding and there and then prayed to the Lord, confessing her sin and the need of God's forgiveness. She also asked Jesus to come into her life and to take over. From that day on Trudy became a totally new person. A few days later she happened to drop into a Catholic Christian Bookshop run by two nuns. Her intention was to become a Roman Catholic, so she thought it would be good to get some Catholic literature. Whilst she was talking to the nuns, a lady from our church family entered the shop. The nuns, by their welcome, obviously knew this lady and jovially enquired, "And what brings you in here today, Marjorie?" To which Marjorie responded, "I don't really know; I just felt the Lord told me to come here." The nuns smiled to each other and said, "Well, we know why. The Lord wants you to take this young lady under your wing and take her along to your church." Trudy began to show steady progress in her walk with the Lord and regularly attended Bible studies organized by Marjorie. After about a year Trudy approached me concerning her marriage. I explained to her that in God's sight she was still married to Fred and that they needed to forgive each other and renew their marriage. In due course I met with Fred who seemed approving of the idea.

It was arranged that they would go away together for a long weekend at a five-star hotel. Their accommodation was a perfect setting with a room overlooking a crystal clear lake that mirrored the surrounding, majestic mountains. The scene was straight out of the travel brochures. Everything seemed to be going well until Fred said, "I'll just pop down to the bar for a box of matches." Fred never returned, at least not for several hours. When Trudy finally went searching for him she found him in the bar the worse for drink. That was the end of their romantic weekend and subsequently their marriage. Fred had no interest in wanting his marriage to work. So long as he had his marijuana, his bottle and the occasional woman he would be content. Eventually, with the full blessing and counsel of the elders, Trudy and Fred were divorced. After three or four years, George, a bachelor in his early thirties enquired of me what I thought about him asking Trudy out for a date. I told him that if he really believed God was in this and he was willing to raise her child as his own, then he would have my blessing. Today, you will find them contentedly married with nine children. They have one of the most loving, disciplined and highly regarded families I know. They also have pastoral responsibility for a flourishing house group.

Elizabeth started coming along to our church family through an invitation from Carol, one of our members with whom she was sharing her marriage problems. She had only been married to Nigel for a few weeks when, to her utter dismay, Nigel informed her that he was gay and was going to leave her to move in with his boyfriend. It was like a bolt out of the blue. Up until this moment she had not the faintest idea that Nigel was a homosexual. Anger and resentment began to take over all her waking hours. She found herself gradually slipping into a deep depression with not the slightest ray of hope. Each time she talked with Carol she would always come away feeling a little uplifted, together with a sense that the future wasn't as bleak as it had first appeared to be. However, once more on her own, the black clouds of despair would return. Elizabeth finally came to the conclusion that unless she handed her life over to the Lord she would not be able to survive.

So it was that one Sunday morning, I was looking out over the congregation and there, to my immense joy, was the sparkling face of Elizabeth beaming back at me. I knew immediately that she was born again. One of the first things she settled was the forgiveness of Nigel. Then there was the issue of their marriage being restored. One of our elders met with Nigel with the hope that he would repent and return to Elizabeth, but Nigel wanted none of it. Not only was he not returning to his wife, he wasn't the slightest bit concerned about getting a divorce – that was up to her! It became abundantly clear to us elders that this marriage needed to be brought to a conclusion. So, one evening Elizabeth, together with her housegroup leaders, joined the elders for a ceremony of releasing her from her marriage vows and to give her our blessing to seek a divorce. As elders, we felt the following position was appropriate for us to take in this particular situation: it was a minister of Christ who had pronounced Nigel and Elizabeth husband and wife, it should, therefore, also be church leaders who pronounced their marriage ended. I prayed a prayer that went something like this: "Lord, we find ourselves saddened by the way in which Nigel has broken and flaunted the breaking of his marriage vows to Elizabeth. We know this grieves Your heart. Nigel has declared he is no longer married to Elizabeth even though she has been willing to receive him back and forgive him. We, therefore, as spiritual leaders release her from this marriage and give her our blessing to bring it to a conclusion through a court of law. We also want to go on record that if, in Your sight Lord Jesus, Elizabeth is wrong in divorcing Nigel, then we also stand equally as guilty." Elizabeth at this point broke down and began to weep. In fact, all of us began to weep. That meeting happened over twenty years ago and I still stand by our decision to bring that marriage to conclusion. Nothing I have read or heard since then has caused me to regret our action.

I'm sure you will have noticed a number of similarities between all three women. Firstly, they were all separated from their husbands at the time of their receiving Christ. Secondly, they all sought out counsel from the elders of the church – in other words they did not act independently. Thirdly, all of them were willing to forgive their husbands and receive them back. Fourthly, each one dealt thoroughly with resentment and bitterness. Fifthly, all three husbands were seen by one or more church elders and all refused to be reconciled to their wives.

Steps of Recovery

If you are currently going through a divorce and want to come out the other side without becoming bitter and hateful, you will need to make some clear choices. Let me offer the following suggestions:

1. Humble yourself. Come to Jesus and tell Him you need His assistance, and simply ask Him to help you. Even if you are not a Christian, He will still come to your aid. If you carry out His instructions found in the Scriptures I think you will be pleasantly surprised with the results.
2. Never entertain self-pity. What you allow into your mind as an overnight guest will rapidly invade and take over every emotional room of your life. Be warned: self-pity, if unchecked, will have a growing destructive influence on all your relationships. Oliver G. Wilson once said, "What poison is to food, self-pity is to life."
3. Ask Jesus to help you to forgive your spouse. Remember, as we mentioned earlier in this book, forgiveness means to "let go" and to "send away".

    "Forgiveness saves the expense of anger, the cost of hatred, the waste of spirits."   (Megiddo Message)

4. Deal severely with the compulsive habit of rehearsing all the wrongs and injustices which you perceive your spouse to have inflicted upon you. If you are now divorced, you need to spend all your emotional energy on coping with the present and planning for the future. Whatever you do, don't let the past rob you of a bright future.
5. Get some counsel from a Bible-believing pastor or minister. Divorce is very similar to bereavement and carries its own grieving process. A minister can be a great spiritual help.
6. Be willing to face the possibility of giving your marriage one more try. It was because John and Jean, who had been separated twice before, decided to phone for help from one of our pastors that I now have a wonderful daughter-in-law. That phone call saved their marriage and brought them to Christ. It also brought their daughter Janet to give her life to Jesus and eventually she and our son Stephen fell in love and were married. Jesus still performs miracles.

7. If there is no alternative to divorce, don't get into acrimonious legal fights – they will only increase your blood pressure and produce a further store of injurious memories.

A Testimony

The following account is how one lady recovered from divorce and was able to face the future.

"Firstly, I want to say that I couldn't have survived this time without God. One of the most important factors in my healing was learning to forgive my ex-husband for all the things he'd done to hurt my family and myself.

I also found that not allowing self-pity any room at all, kept me from getting bitter and I also reminded myself there are plenty of people a lot worse off than myself.

One of the major things I have been learning through all this difficult time is to be content with what I have got and make the best of things as they are. Joining the church that I am now in also played a major part in my recovery. Here I began learning about God, benefited from the fellowship of good, loving people and put everything I had into worshipping God. It also helped by healing my distrust in men. I had begun to think some years ago that most men (with the exception of a very few) were a race apart and not to be trusted, but gradually, as I got to know the married couples in our church, I realized that there were still men that were good and could be trusted.

Slowly, I am being healed of all my wrong thinking and I'm feeling ready to face the future, full of optimism. This time spent on my own has been precious to me, to build up a real relationship with God. Now I can feel a 'whole' person with all my security rooted in Jesus who will never let me down, so that if I should meet a godly man that I could marry, I am now so secure in God that I feel I could have a healthy, balanced relationship with whoever I was to marry – not trying to find all my happiness and security in him, but in God first and foremost.

But if it is not God's will for me to remarry, my life as a Christian is so rich and exciting that I know I will be able to cope. God says that He has come to bring us life, life in abundance. Thanks to God, that is what I have – life in abundance."

To all of you who are struggling with your marriage; to all those who are presently separated from your spouse and are facing divorce, and to all who have been divorced, I trust that this chapter may have been of particular help. I pray that you may have the will, faith and humility to off-load all of your hurt, anxiety, hopelessness and disappointment onto Jesus. We read in 1 Peter 5:6–7,

> *"Therefore humble yourselves under the mighty hand of God, that He may exalt you at the proper time, casting all your anxiety on Him, because He cares for you."*

We can be absolutely confident that Jesus carries our concerns in His heart at all times. Even if we think no one else cares, we can rest assured that He has not forgotten us. Jesus said in Luke 12:6–7,

> *"Are not five sparrows sold for two cents? Yet not one of them is forgotten before God. Indeed, the very hairs of your head are all numbered. Do not fear; you are of more value than many sparrows."*

Let me conclude by giving you these blessings from the Scriptures:

> *"My God shall supply all your needs according to His riches in glory in Christ Jesus."*   (Philippians 4:19)

> *"Now may our Lord Jesus Christ Himself and God our Father, who has loved us and given us eternal comfort and good hope by grace, comfort and strengthen your hearts in every good work and word."*   (2 Thessalonians 2:16–17)

And finally,

> *"The LORD bless you, and keep you;*
> *The LORD make His face shine on you,*
> *And be gracious to you;*
> *The LORD lift up His countenance on you,*
> *And give you peace."*   (Numbers 6:24–26)

Amen.

Conclusion

In the preface at the beginning of this book, I promised that the answers I would offer would all find their rationale from the Scriptures and ultimately be centered in the Lord Jesus. How successful I have been in this endeavor must be left to your judgment. However, I do want to emphasize this point again in closing: Jesus is at the center of the answer to all of our needs. The Scriptures tell us that He is full of grace and truth; He is meek and lowly of heart; He has all authority in heaven and on earth and all the treasures of wisdom and knowledge are hidden in Him. The answer to all of our problems is Jesus Christ Himself, as L.H. Edmonds wrote:

> "My faith has found a resting place,
>   not in device nor creed;
> I trust the ever-living one,
>   his wounds for me shall plead."

Jesus Himself, is the greatest treasure of all. In coming to Christ we are coming to the source of everything. It is of vital importance that we grasp the truth that faith is the key, and the only key, that will unlock to us Christ's treasures. Doing religious things won't open the door, nor will trusting in our own goodness, for there is no other way to come to God but by believing that Jesus is God and that He is the rewarder of those who seek Him. The bolt that holds those treasures locked and unattainable is our unbelief. Even Jesus could do no mighty work because of the unbelief in the hearts of the inhabitants of His own home town. If we are going to break through to use the key of faith, then we must be assertive, even warlike, in combating faithlessness – the arch-enemy of our faith. Our response can not be better put than that written in John Newton's great hymn:

"Begone unbelief; my Savior is near,
And for my relief will surely appear:
By prayer let me wrestle, and he will perform;
With Christ in the vessel, I smile at the storm.

Though dark be my way, since he is my guide,
'Tis mine to obey, 'tis his to provide:
Though cisterns be broken and creatures all fail,
The word he has spoken shall surely prevail.

His love in time past forbids me to think
He'll leave me at last in trouble to sink;
While each Ebenezer I have in review
Confirms his good pleasure to help me quite through.

Why should I complain of want or distress,
Temptation or pain? He told me no less;
The heirs of salvation, I know from his word,
Through much tribulation must follow their Lord.

Since all that I meet shall work for my good,
The bitter is sweet, the medicine food;
Though painful at present, 'twill cease before long;
And then O how pleasant the conqueror's song!"